ILEX FOUNDATION SERIES 23

ONOMASTIC REFORMS

Also in the Ilex Foundation Series

Dreaming across Boundaries: The Interpretation of Dreams in Islamic Lands
edited by Louise Marlow

Strī: Women in Epic Mahābhārata
by Kevin McGRATH

Persian Literature and Judeo-Persian Culture: Collected Writings of Sorour S. Soroudi
edited by H. E. Chehabi

The Rhetoric of Biography: Narrating Lives in Persianate Societies
edited by L. Marlow

Jaya: Performance in Epic Mahābhārata
by Kevin McGRATH

The History *of Beyhaqi (The History of Sultan Masʿud of Ghazna, 1030–1041) by Abu'l-Fażl Beyhaqi*
translated and with commentaries by Clifford Edmund Bosworth
fully revised and with further commentary by Mohsen Ashtiany

The Last of the Rephaim: Conquest and Cataclysm in the Heroic Ages of Ancient Israel
by Brian R. Doak

Ruse and Wit: The Humorous in Arabic, Turkish, and Persian Narrative
edited by Dominic Parvis Brookshaw

Kṛṣṇa: Friendship in Epic Mahābhārata
by Kevin McGRATH

On the Wonders of Land and Sea: Persianate Travel Writing
edited by Roberta Micallef and Sunil Sharma

Poet and Hero in the Persian Book of Kings
third edition
by Olga M. Davidson

Comparative Literature and Classical Persian Poetics
second edition
by Olga M. Davidson

Ferdowsi's Shāhnāma: *Millennial Perspectives*
edited by Olga M. Davidson and Marianna Shreve Simpson

Mirror of Dew: The Poetry of Ālam-tāj Zhāle Qā'em-Maqāmi
translated with an introduction by Asghar Seyed-Gohrab

Global Medieval: Mirrors for Princes Reconsidered
edited by Regula Forster and Neguin Yavari

Erin and Iran: Cultural Encounters between the Irish and the Iranians
edited by H. E. Chehabi and Grace Neville

ONOMASTIC REFORMS

FAMILY NAMES AND STATE BUILDING IN IRAN

H. E. Chehabi

Ilex Foundation
Boston, Massachusetts

Distributed by Harvard University Press
Cambridge, Massachusetts and London, England

Onomastic Reforms: Family Names and State Building in Iran
by H. E. Chehabi

Published by Ilex Foundation, Boston, Massachusetts

Distributed by Harvard University Press, Cambridge, Massachusetts and London, England

Production editor: Christopher Dadian
Cover design: Joni Godlove
Printed in the United States of America

Cover image: "Tashkhiṣ va tarqim-e alqāb," 1862. Published in *Farhang-e Irānzamin* 19 (1352/1973).

ISBN: 9780674248199

Library of Congress Control Number: 2020037953

For Farhad, Farrokh, Najmedin, Siamak,
and to the memory of Kavous,
the first friends with whom I was on first-name terms

CONTENTS

PREFACE

NAMES HAVE FASCINATED ME FOR A LONG TIME. My first experience with state regulations regarding names was shortly after I was born, when my father had to bribe a registry official in Tehran to record a second given name for me – thanks to which I now have something to put in the space marked "middle name" on American forms. My onomastic identity was also shaped by informal conventions that I myself, later in life, found to be not self-evident: In spite of having had a German mother, I have no German given name, and as a religiously indifferent teenager I was somewhat bemused to learn that I had a Muslim *tu-gushi* (literally "in-the-ear") name recorded in the family Koran.[1]

Growing up as a quasi-monolingual German speaker in Tehran, I knew my cousins and the children of my parents' friends by their first names, but when, as a five-year-old, I was sent to a Persian-medium school, I very quickly learned to address the other boys in my class by their family names – which seemed odd in the beginning. This practice continued in high school, except with my bosom buddies. That naming conventions are social constructs is, therefore, something I intuited early in life. That names also have a class dimension was brought home to me decades later, when I found myself at the grave of my father's nanny in Kerman and saw her family name engraved on the tombstone. I had heard about her all my life but always referred to simply by her given name, and it had simply not occurred to me, as a child, to enquire after the surnames of domestic staff.

A few years ago, the project of a festschrift for Amin Banani allowed me to indulge my fascination with names. His book on the reforms instituted during the reign of Reżā Shah Pahlavi had been my first introduction to the changes in the fabric of everyday life brought about by Iran's modernizers after World War I,[2] and so I devoted my contribution to the festschrift to the introduction of family names and the abolition of titles in Iran.[3] Much of the research for that article was done in February 2006 at the home of

1. These are names derived from the Muslim tradition that are informally given to a newborn whose officially registered given name is not Islamic. They are somewhat analogous to the "Hebrew names" of Jews.

2. Amin Banani, *The Modernization of Iran* (Stanford: Stanford University Press, 1961).

3. H. E. Chehabi, "The Reform of Iranian Nomenclature and Titulature in the Fifth Majles," in Wali Ahmadi, ed., *Convergent Zones: Persian Literary Tradition and the Writing of History: Studies in Honor of Amin Banani* (Costa Mesa, CA: Mazda Publishers, 2012), 84–116. I thank Mazda Publishers for allowing me to recycle passages from that article.

Mohamad Tavakoli-Targhi in Toronto, and I remain grateful for his gracious permission to use his vast collection of newspapers and journals.

When Florian Schwarz, the director of the Institute of Iranian Studies of the Austrian Academy of Sciences (which had hosted me during a sabbatical year in 2004–2005 at the invitation of its then director, Bert Fragner), honored me with an invitation to deliver the keynote address at the celebration of the Institute's tenth anniversary in April, 2013, I settled on the topic of *Die Einführung von Familiennamen in Iran in den 1920er Jahren* as an homage to the Institute's monumental research project on Iranian onomastics.[4] To prepare for that address, I spent a fortnight doing additional research at the Institute's library, where Sibylle Wentker saw to it that I had all the resources that I needed. In Vienna, it was Velizar Sadovski who first broached the possibility of turning my research into a little book. I thank all the scholars at the Institute for their friendship and encouragement over the years.

In the course of writing this book I have received editorial help, genealogical information, and substantive feedback from Shademan Akhavan, Mehrdad Amanat, Gulnora Aminova, Reza Azari Shahrezai, Erik Goldstein, Maryam Kamali, Hasan Kayalı, Ahmad Mahdavi Damghani, Louise Marlow, Guive Mirfendereski, Behnaz Mirzai, Hassan Mneimneh, John Perry, Behrang Rajabi, Maryam Salour, Homa Sarshar, Sunil Sharma, Abolala Soudavar, Fatema Soudavar, Amin Tarzi, Farzin Vahdat, and Heidi Walcher. Oliver Bast, Ali Gheissari, Arang Keshavarzian, Rudi Matthee, David Motadel, Roy P. Mottahedeh, and Yann Richard read the entire manuscript and provided me with detailed comments. Marie Deer copyedited the manuscript with her habitual skill and precision and created verse translations for the poems quoted in the book. I am very grateful to all of them. A summer fellowship from the Alexander-von-Humboldt Foundation allowed me to finish the bulk of the project as a guest of the Zentrum Moderner Orient in Berlin in the summer of 2015, and I thank both institutions for their generosity.

4. See Rüdiger Schmitt, *Das iranische Personen-Namenbuch: Rückschau, Vorschau, Rundschau* (Vienna: Verlag der Österreichischen Akademie der Wissenschaften, 2006).

1

INTRODUCTION

BETWEEN 1918 AND 1935, the Iranian state established a unified onomastic regime for all Iranians.[1] This took the form of laws, some issued by the cabinet and others resulting from parliamentary legislation, as well as decrees regulating minor issues. Analytically, four distinct measures can be distinguished in Iran, although in practice and in public perception they have more often than not been conflated.

The first, and arguably most important, measure was the establishment of official registries in 1918, called *sejell-e aḥvāl* until 1935 and *s̱abt-e aḥvāl* thereafter,[2] where all Iranians were required to register their names and where the particulars of their personal status – birth, marriage, divorce, and death – were kept. In return, they received a document containing the information (and later a photo), which would thenceforth serve as their certificate of identity and citizenship for all transactions involving the state. The second measure was the introduction of family names. Iranians, which in practice meant Iranian men, were first invited and then required to adopt a second name, termed *shohrat, nām-e khānevādegi*, or *esm-e fāmil(i)*, i.e., "family name," which they would pass on to their descendants. The third measure was the abolition of titles, *elghā'-e alqāb*. Honorary titles (which were in theory non-hereditary) were bestowed on ostensibly meritorious men and women by the Shah, and the abolition of those titles by an act of parliament in 1925 was part of the toppling of the Qājār dynasty and of the inegalitarian ancien régime that modernist reformers associated with it. The fourth and last measure was the regulation of honorifics, *'anāvin* (pl. of *'onvān*), most of which were banned from public use while a few were standardized. This regulation was done in stages and completed by 1935.

The standardization of naming practices was a worldwide phenomenon, made necessary by the development of the modern bureaucratic state.[3] But

1. Quite a few towns and even provinces also had their names changed in those and subsequent years, but that is beyond the scope of this study.

2. Doktor Ḥoseyn Maḥbubi Ardakāni, *Tārikh-e mo'assesāt-e tamaddoni-ye jadid dar Irān*, volume 2 (Tehran: Mo'asseseh-ye Enteshārāt va Chāp-e Dāneshgāh-e Tehrān, 1376/1998), 160.

3. C.A. Bayly, *The Birth of the Modern World 1780–1914* (Oxford: Blackwell, 2004), 18.

there is no compelling reason why the four measures listed above should necessarily go together. As we will see below, this can best be illustrated by adducing examples from other countries, especially non-Western states that, like Iran, maintained their formal sovereignty in the age of imperialism but whose leaders felt pressured to conform to European practices in order to safeguard their nation's fragile sovereignty: China, Japan, Siam/Thailand, the Ottoman Empire/Turkey, and Abyssinia/Ethiopia.

In Europe itself, state registries had an antecedent in the parish registries that recorded personal status. In France, it was in the aftermath of the 1789 revolution that the state established centralized registries,[4] one motivation being the wish of the new holders of power to diminish the social influence of the Roman Catholic clergy. The establishment of a centralized civil registry system was thus an expression of both state building and secularization.[5] Over the course of the nineteenth century, other European countries followed France's lead. Beginning in the 1820s, the Ottoman Empire instituted registries in stages, in conjunction with censuses, for ever-growing segments of the population.[6] In Japan, registries were also connected with censuses and had a history reaching back to the sixth century, but a modern, nationwide registration system, *koseki*, was established in 1872, only four years after the Meiji Restoration laid the foundations for a centralized state. While the *koseki* did away with earlier rigid status distinctions and aimed to register all inhabitants of Japan in a standardized way, individuals were only registered as members of a household unit (which is still the case today).[7]

As far as family names are concerned, the concept of a heritable second name is by no means universal, and to this day many countries do not require their citizens to carry one; in Iceland they are even forbidden as per a law promulgated in 1925 to resist Danification, at a time when the island was an autonomous territory within the Kingdom of Denmark.[8] What most Icelanders have as a second name is a patronym, i.e., the father's name, to which *son* (son) or *dottir* (daughter) is added. In China, meanwhile, the use of the same, shared second name by people united by a common lineage

4. Gérard Noiriel, "The Identification of the Citizen: The Birth of Republican Civil Status in France," in Jane Caplan and John Torpey, eds., *Documenting Individual Identity: The Development of State Practices in the Modern World* (Princeton: Princeton University Press, 2001), 28–48.

5. For a detailed account of the various measures in France see Anne Lefebvre-Teillard, *Le nom: droit et histoire* (Paris: Presses universitaires de France, 1990), 113–131.

6. Stanford J. Shaw, "The Ottoman Census System and Population, 1831–1914," *International Journal of Middle East Studies* 9:3 (October 1978): 325–338.

7. Kenji Mori, "The Development of the Modern *koseki*," in David Chapman and Karl Jakob Krogness, eds., *Japan's Household Registration System and Citizenship:* Koseki, *Identification and Documentation* (London: Routledge, 2014), 59–75.

8. Richard F. Tomasson, "The Continuity of Icelandic Names and Naming Patterns," *Names* 23:4 (December 1975): 281.

began in ancient times; this second name long ago acquired the function of the family name.[9] In Europe, finally, centuries before the establishment of registries, family names developed from epithets or nicknames used to distinguish between two or more individuals who bore the same name. It was in Venice that such nicknames or bynames first became hereditary in the ninth century, and from Venice the practice of carrying a hereditary second name spread to the rest of the European continent and, in 1066, on to Great Britain with the Norman Conquest.[10] In the last centuries of the ancien regime, they became so prevalent in France that the word *nom*, which had hitherto meant "given name," came to mean "surname."[11]

In Japan, in theory, only the higher orders of society (such as the samurai) were entitled to family names until 1870, when the Meiji government allowed all Japanese to register a surname. The obligation to do so followed five years later, with a new law in 1875.[12] In Thailand, family names were made obligatory in 1913.[13] In Turkey, provision for surnames was made in the Turkish Civil Code of 1926, but they became obligatory only in 1934.[14] In Ethiopia, a person's second name was traditionally his or her father's first name,[15] and although the Ethiopian Civil Code of 1960 stipulated that "[e]very Ethiopian ... must have a family name,"[16] hereditary surnames did not catch on except among the diaspora. Contemporary Ethiopian bureaucratic rules require that an individual's identification card contain name, father's name, and grandfather's name.[17]

As for colonies, while hereditary surnames were introduced here and there by the imperial authorities, this was not done consistently or for all colonial subjects. In Algeria, for instance, when civil registries were first established by the French colonial authorities, they recorded only the traditional names. Surnames were made obligatory in 1873 for Algerians who wanted to register property and in 1882–1883 for the rest of the indigenous

9. Russell Jones, *Chinese Names: The Traditions Surrounding the Use of Chinese Surnames and Personal Names* (Selangor: Pelanduk Publications, 1997), 1–11.

10. Sylvie Nautré, *Le nom en droit comparé* (Frankfurt: Peter Lang, 1977), 10–14.

11. Lefebvre-Teillard, *Le nom*, 56.

12. Herbert Plutschow, *Japan's Name Culture: The Significance of Names in a Religious, Political and Social Context* (Sandgate: Japan Library, 1995), 192–193.

13. Chris Baker and Pasuk Phongpaichit, *A History of Thailand*, 2nd ed. (Melbourne: Cambridge University Press, 2009), 97.

14. Meltem Türköz, *Naming and Nation-building in Turkey: The 1934 Surname Law* (New York: PalgraveMacmillan, 2018), 64–79.

15. Elias Yemane, *Amharic and Ethiopic Onomastics: A Classic Ethiopian Legacy, Concept, and Ingenuity* (Lewsiton: The Edwin Mellen Press, 2004), 33.

16. Jacques Vanderlinden, *The Law of Physical Persons (Art. 1-393). Commentaries upon the Ethiopian Civil Code* (Addis Abeba: Faculty of Law, Haile Sellassie I University, 1969), 21–28.

17. *Encyclopaedia Aethiopica*, s.v. "Names" (by Steven Kaplan and Wolbert Smidt).

population. The governor general sent special commissars to the various communes, where they convoked meetings of the heads of Algerian families to register their family names – those who did not appear were simply assigned one. In exchange, they were given identity documents.[18] In Nigeria, the British gave indigenous military recruits surnames derived from their places of origin.[19]

Titles are usually associated with traditional forms of governance and are often abolished after a revolution. In the United States, Article 6 of the Articles of Confederation of 1781 stipulates that the "United States in Congress assembled, or any of them, [shall not] grant any title of nobility," a prohibition reiterated in Article 1, Section 9 of the United States Constitution of 1787. The French revolutionaries followed suit, but titles were reintroduced under Napoleon. Communists did away with titles in the European countries where they took power. So did the Austrian republicans in 1919, but in Germany, following the fall of the monarchies in 1918, titles were incorporated into surnames.[20]

As for honorifics, they are used both formally and informally in most societies, ranging from "His Honor" for an American mayor to the *sensei* that is appended to a teacher's name in Japan. Honorifics are often used in correspondence as well, as when a letter is addressed to *El Excelentísimo y Ilustrísimo Señor Don* Fulano de Tal in Spain, although legally a more restrictive (and very detailed) code governs the use of honorifics in that country.[21] In Turkey, honorifics were abolished a few months after the introduction of obligatory family names in November 1934.[22]

The contemporaneity of the measures enumerated above in the Iranian case can be explained by the urgency that attached to state building in Iran in the years after World War I, an urgency that was due to both external and internal circumstances.

The Challenges of the "Standard of Civilization"

In the long nineteenth century, Iran was one of only half a dozen or so non-Western states that were not incorporated into one of the European empires.

18. E.-H. Perreau, *Le Droit au nom en matière civile* (Paris: Librairie de la Société du Recueil Sirey, 1910), 298–299.

19. Paul Delmond, "De l'imposition des noms de personnes aux africains," *Bulletin de l'Institut Français d'Afrique Noire* 15:2 (1953): 460.

20. For details, see Nautré, *Le nom en droit comparé*, 96–101.

21. For details see *Wikipedia* (Spanish), s.v. "Anexo: Tratamientos oficiales en España," https://es.wikipedia.org/wiki/Anexo:Tratamientos_oficiales_en_Espa%C3%B1a. Accessed on 25 November 2016.

22. *Oriente Moderno* 14:12 (December 1934): 576–577.

One of the most notable of these was the Ottoman Empire, which, as the only other Muslim power and Iran's immediate neighbor, has particular relevance for comparative purposes. While these states remained formally sovereign, they were not considered equals by the Great Powers, who forced them to accept nonreciprocal obligations referred to as "unequal treaties." The most important of these unequal treaties were the "capitulations," arrangements that exempted subjects of the Western countries from the jurisdiction of local courts. The justification given by the capitulatory powers for retaining jurisdiction over their subjects was that the non-Western countries lacked adequate legal systems, as a consequence of which a European could not expect fair treatment in their courts.[23] Countries like Iran were therefore in a liminal situation: they were neither colonies, where the Europeans could impose their laws on everybody, nor fully sovereign states, whose laws applied to all who resided in their territory. As the German/British jurist Lassa Francis Lawrence Oppenheim, whom many regard the father of the modern discipline of international law, put it in his classic textbook of international law, "Persia, Siam, China, Abyssinia, and the like were certainly civilised states ... but their civilisation has not yet reached that condition which is necessary to enable their Government and their populations in every respect to understand and to carry out the command of the rule of International Law."[24] They were referred to as "semi-civilized,"[25] which was a convenient way to justify outside interference in their affairs short of depriving them of formal sovereignty. Naturally, local elites endeavored to put an end to this inequality by reforming their countries so as to meet the Westerners' "standard of civilization."[26] This involved not only creating new institutions modeled on those of the evidently successful West, but also cultural borrowing that would render individuals more "civilized" in the eyes of the Europeans and "modern" in their own eyes.[27]

23. For a discussion of Persia, Siam, the Ottoman Empire, and Japan, see Yaotong Tchen, *De la disparition de la jurisdiction consulaire dans certains pays d'Orient* (Paris: Les Presses Modernes, 1931); for China, see Kouo Kin Yao, *La Chine et les capitulations* (Nancy: Imprimerie Georges Thomas, 1938).

24. L. Oppenheim, *International Law: A Treatise* (London: Longman's, 1905), 33.

25. Their liminal situation found expression in other realms of analysis as well. Lenin, for instance, referred to these states as "semi-colonies" since they were subjected to economic penetration by Western powers. See V. I. Lenin, "On the Slogan for the United States of Europe," *Collected Works*, volume 21 (New York: International Publishers, 1967), 339–343.

26. See Gerrit W. Gong, *The Standard of 'Civilization' in International Society* (Oxford: Clarendon Press, 1984), which includes chapters on China, Japan, Siam, Ethiopia, and the Ottoman Empire, but not Persia.

27. For Iran, see Rouzbeh Parsi, *In Search of Caravans Lost: Iranian Intellectuals and Nationalist Discourse in the Inter-War Years* (Lund: Media-tryck, 2009), where "caravan" refers to the "caravan of civilization" that had left Iran behind, a favorite trope of Iranian modernists. For Siam,

In the nineteenth century, the use of family names was deemed to be one such outward sign of civilization. As a French treatise on names had it, the "necessity to distinguish each individual gave birth to proper names; but with all the ancient peoples, the Romans excepted, as well as with the Arabs and *not yet civilized modern peoples*, hereditary names were and still are unknown." It went on to aver that the "use of hereditary names" was "one of the most necessary elements of the regular constitution of a civilized people," and observed that the "use of family names does not exist yet among the Arabs, the Turks, and *the Persians*."[28]

Similar attitudes could also be found outside Europe. In 1910 an article appeared in an English-language newspaper in Bangkok that suggested that surnames constituted "one of the signs by which one may judge of the progress of civilization in a people," and that in this area Siamese civilization could stand improvement.[29] And in 1924, a decade before family names were made obligatory in Turkey, the modernist ideologue Ziya Gökalp wrote that "[i]n every civilized nation there is a title for each family that usually comes after the personal name," as a consequence of which "each family should be asked to take a family name."[30] As we shall see, Iranian reformers held views much like these. But first let us take a brief look at the specific circumstances that conditioned their attempts to meet the "standard of civilization" – onomastic or otherwise.

Iran in the First Quarter of the Twentieth Century

Iranians became conscious of their weakness vis-à-vis the European powers when the Russian forces defeated Iranian armies in the first three decades of the nineteenth century, leading to the Treaty of Turkmenchay, in 1828, which for the first time imposed capitulations on Iran. Soon other European

---

see Thongchai Winichakul, "The Quest for 'Siwilai': A Geographical Discourse of Civilizational Thinking in the Late Nineteenth and Early Twentieth-Century Siam," *The Journal of Asian Studies* 59:3 (August 2000): 528–549, where *siwilai* is the Thai word derived from "civilization."

28. [François Gilbert,] Baron de Coston, *Origine, étymologie & signification des noms propres et des armoiries* (Paris: Chez Aug. Aubry, éditeur, 1867), 10, 15, 32. My translation; emphasis added. (Please note that from here on, unless otherwise noted, translations are my own.) As late as 1959, a book on English surnames began with the words: "In many parts of the world there are no such things as surnames at all: primitive communities, where everyone knows everyone else, and there is little travel, do not need them." James Pennethorne Hughes, *How You Got Your Name: The Origin and Meaning of Surnames* (London: Phoenix House, 1959), 7.

29. *Bangkok Times*, 12 August 1910, as quoted in Walter F. Vella, *Chaiyo!: King Vajiravudh and the Development of Thai Nationalism* (Honolulu: The University Press of Hawaii, 1978), 129.

30. *Cumhuriyet*, 27 May 1924, as quoted in Türköz, *Naming and Nation-building in Turkey*, 39–40. Note that Gökalp already used a surname.

countries obtained capitulations as well.[31] As a buffer state between Czarist Russia in the north and the British Empire in the south, Iran maintained a precarious formal independence, punctuated by competitive meddling in its domestic affairs by the two powers.[32] "Civilized" status was associated with constitutionalism, a view confirmed when in the Russo-Japanese War of 1904–1905 the only constitutionalist state in Asia defeated the only European state without a constitution, a victory that sent shock waves through Asia.[33] When Iran became a constitutional monarchy in 1906, therefore (following a revolution), Iranian reformers hoped that this would enhance Iran's sovereignty, but the opposite happened: in the Anglo-Russian Convention of 1907, Britain and Russia agreed to divide the country into two "spheres of influence" (with a neutral zone in between), thereby depriving Iran's leaders of the little political leeway they had previously been able to maintain by playing one power against the other.[34]

The external environment became ever more threatening to Iran's sovereignty after that. By 1909, key parts of northern Iran were under Russian occupation. In the south, British anxieties about maintaining communications with India led to a large British presence. The stationing of Russian troops in the north of Iran led to battles between these and Ottoman armies during World War I in northwestern Iran, while local levies raised and commanded by the British were skirmishing with tribal forces in southern Iran that were allied with the Central Powers. Neither the Triple Entente nor the Central Powers respected Iran's neutrality, but Russian troops left northern Iran after the outbreak of the Bolshevik revolution in 1917, only to be replaced by British ones. The adverse effects on the local population of foreign troops battling on a neutral country's territory were devastating.[35] To add insult to injury, when the Iranian government sent a delegation to the Paris Peace Conference to request reparations for the damage done by warring

31. For an overview, see Guive Mirfendereski, *The Privileged American: The U.S. Capitulations in Iran 1856–79* (Costa Mesa, CA: Mazda Publishers, 2014), 10–21.

32. Firuz Kazemzadeh, *Russia and Britain in Persia, 1864–1914: A Study in Imperialism* (New Haven: Yale University Press, 1968).

33. Rotem Kowner, ed., *The Impact of the Russo-Japanese War* (London: Routledge, 2007). For a detailed discussion of the constitutional revolutions that followed, see Charles Kurzman, *Democracy Denied, 1905–1915: Intellectuals and the Fate of Democracy* (Cambridge, MA: Harvard University Press, 2008).

34. Rogers Platt Churchill, *The Anglo-Russian Convention of 1907* (Cedar Rapids, IA: The Torch Press, 1939), 212–268.

35. Kaveh Ehsani, "Oil, State and Society in Iran in the Aftermath of the First World War," in Thomas Fraser, ed., *The First World War and its Aftermath* (London & Chicago: Gingko Library Press, 2015), 191–212.

foreign armies on its soil, the Iranians were not admitted to the conference on the pretext that the country had not been a belligerent.[36]

After Iran's constitutional revolution of 1905–1906, Iranian governments began the task of state building in earnest.[37] At the most basic level, this meant creating institutions that would assure the state a monopoly of the legitimate use of physical force, to use Max Weber's formulation.[38] The foundations of a modern judiciary were laid,[39] and a police force and gendarmerie were created.[40] The modern educational system expanded,[41] its graduates staffing the new institutions. And to pay for the creation of a modern centralized state, public finances had to be reformed, which was perhaps the most difficult task, given people's natural disinclination to be taxed.

The practical results of these efforts, however, were disappointing. Chronic internecine political rivalries and ideological conflicts at the center, challenges to the central government's authority by rival pretenders to the throne, and a perennially empty treasury were the main causes. In December 1910 the government hired a foreign treasury expert, the American W. Morgan Shuster, to put order into Iranian finances, but when in 1911 he tried to seize the property of two rebel princes who enjoyed Russian protection, the Russians threatened to march on Tehran if he was not dismissed, and the government acceded to their ultimatum.[42] In the following years, cabinets were short-lived, tribes were armed and restive, bandits terrorized the countryside, and the government gradually lost control over large parts of the Iranian territory.[43] To top it all off, about one Iranian in ten (close to a million people) died when the global influenza pandemic arrived in Iran, affecting a

36. Oliver Bast, "La mission persane à la Conférence de Paix en 1919: une nouvelle interprétation," in Oliver Bast, ed., *La Perse et la Grande Guerre* (Tehran/Paris: Institut Français de Recherche en Iran/Peeters, 2002), 375–426; and Bast, "Putting the Record Straight: Vosuq al-Dowleh's Foreign Policy in 1918/19," in Touraj Atabaki and Erik J. Zürcher, eds., *Men of Order: Authoritarian Modernization under Atatürk and Reza Shah* (London: I.B. Tauris, 2004), 260–281.

37. Omid Uskowi and A. Reza Sheikholeslami, "Impact of the Constitutional Revolution on the Development of the Modern State in Iran," in Wali Ahmadi, ed. *Convergent Zones: Persian Literary Tradition and the Writing of History: Studies in Honor of Amin Banani* (Costa Mesa, CA: Mazda Publishers, 2012), 117–148.

38. Max Weber, *Economy and Society*, trans. Guenther Roth and Claus Wittich (Berkeley: California University Press, 1978), 54.

39. Hadi Enayat, *Law, State, and Society in Modern Iran: Constitutionalism, Autocracy, and Legal Reform, 1906-1941* (New York: Palgrave Macmillan, 2013), 83–112.

40. Stephanie Cronin, *The Army and the Creation of the Pahlavi State in Iran, 1910-1926* (London: I.B. Tauris, 1997), 17–53.

41. David Menashri, *Education and the Making of Modern Iran* (Ithaca, NY: Cornell University Press, 1992), 6–79.

42. W. Morgan Shuster, *The Strangling of Persia* (1912, Washington, DC: Mage, 1987).

43. For greater detail see Homa Katouzian, *State and Society in Iran: The Eclipse of the Qajars and the Emergence of the Pahlavis* (London: I.B. Tauris, 2006), 55–87.

population already weakened by famine and an outbreak of typhoid fever.[44] By 1918, most of Iran's politicians and public opinion leaders were united in the conviction that the country needed to be restored to a tolerable degree of order and discipline – with or without respect for constitutional niceties.[45] As Bert Fragner has argued, World War I was a turning point in modern Iranian history, as it laid bare the country's weaknesses and paved the way for widespread acceptance of the notion that drastic and forceful action was needed to address Iran's problems.[46]

In late July 1918, Mirzā Ḥasan Khān Vos̱uq al-Dowleh (Assurance of the State), an experienced statesman in whom reformers had vested their hopes and who enjoyed wide support across all major political factions, was asked by the sovereign, Aḥmad Shah (r. 1909–1925), to become prime minister. Vos̱uq al-Dowleh's tenure lasted nearly two years, longer than that of any of his predecessors. He set to his task energetically, but his reform efforts were hampered by insufficient financial resources. To remedy the situation, he signed a treaty with Great Britain that, while maintaining Iran's sovereignty, would grant the British an exclusive role in developing the capacities of the Iranian state in exchange for a loan of £2 million, but public opinion in Iran deemed the agreement prejudicial to Iran's independence.[47] The treaty was not implemented and Vos̱uq al-Dowleh resigned. More short-lived cabinets followed until, in February 1921, the country's main military force, the Cossack Division, carried out a coup d'état, presented by its perpetrators as a strike against the old establishment. In his first declaration, Seyyed Ẓiyā al-Din Ṭabāṭabā'i, the civilian leader of the coup whom Aḥmad Shah named prime minister, declared:

> A few hundred rich aristocrats, who had taken the reins of the country in a hereditary way, have sucked the nation's blood like leeches,... [and] have filled the political and social life of our homeland with corruption.... The time has come to ... end the rule of this class.[48]

It is no coincidence that the agitation against titles started, as we shall see, after this coup.

Seyyed Ẓiyā was soon sidelined by the commander of the Cossack

44. Amir Arsalan Afkhami, "Compromised Constitutions: The Iranian Experience with the 1918 Influenza Pandemic," *Bulletin of the History of Medicine* 77:2 (Summer 2003): 367–392.

45. Katouzian, *State and Society in Iran*, 88.

46. Bert Fragner, "World War I as a Turning Point in Iranian History," in Bast, ed., *La Perse et la Grande Guerre*, 443–447.

47. Homa Katouzian, "The Campaign Against the Anglo-Iranian Agreement of 1919," *British Journal of Middle Eastern Studies* 25:1 (1998): 5–46.

48. Bāqer 'Āqeli, *Ruzshomār-e tārikh-e Irān az mashruṭeh tā enqelāb-e eslāmi* (Tehran: Nashr-e Goftār, 1369/1990), 382.

Division, Reżā Khān Pahlavi, who assumed more and more power in the course of a creeping regime change that culminated in the abolition of the Qājār dynasty in 1925 and Reżā Pahlavi's coronation as the new shah in 1926. The political history of this era is outside the compass of this study;[49] what matters for our purposes is that there are considerable continuities between the reform measures undertaken before and after the 1921 coup, continuities that political histories with their "emphasis on reigns, regimes, and real or imagined landmarks"[50] often conceal. What did change after 1921 was that oil revenues increased significantly,[51] giving the state the means actually to implement many measures envisaged before the coup.

We have seen that the introduction of hereditary family names was an act of acculturation to European practices, and that at the end of World War I state building was a matter of life or death for Iranians. Let us now examine how the two were connected.

State Building and Surnames

The standardization of naming practices has historically, in most parts of the world, gone hand in hand with state building.[52] Standardization implies the external agency of a centralized state, whose officials, in order to discharge their duties, need to have detailed information on all the people who reside in the state's territory. The first step is to count the inhabitants, after which the information obtained in the census is collected and centrally recorded, the purpose of the exercise being to simplify "the classic state functions of taxation, conscription, and prevention of rebellion."[53] The link between censuses, taxation, and conscription was manifest in the Ottoman Empire,[54] and in Japan "officials could not conceive of a conscription army without giving a surname to all recruits."[55] In fact, the 1875 law mentioned

49. For detailed accounts see Katouzian, *State and Society in Iran*; and Cyrus Ghani, *Iran and the Rise of Reza Shah: From Qajar Collapse to Pahlavi Rule* (London: I.B. Tauris, 1998).

50. In the words of Hasan Kayalı, "Liberal Practices in the Transformation from Empire to Nation-State: The Rump Ottoman Empire, 1918–1923," in Christoph Schumann, ed., *Liberal Thought in the Eastern Mediterranean: Late 19th Century until the 1960s* (Leiden: Brill, 2008), 175.

51. Homa Katouzian, *The Political Economy of Modern Iran: Despotism and Pseudo-Despotism, 1926–1979* (London: Macmillan, 1981), 93.

52. James C. Scott, John Tehranian, and Jeremy Mathias, "The Production of Legal Identities Proper to States: The Case of the Permanent Family Name," *Comparative Studies in Society and History* 44:1 (January 2002): 4–44.

53. James C. Scott, *Seeing Like a State: How Certain Schemes to Improve the Human Condition Have Failed* (New Haven: Yale University Press, 1998), 2.

54. See, for instance, Veysel Şimşek, "The First 'Little Mehmeds': Conscripts for the Ottoman Army, 1826–53," *Osmanlı Araştırmaları / The Journal of Ottoman Studies* 44 (2014): 265–311. See also Shaw, "The Ottoman Census System."

55. Plutschow, *Japan's Name Culture*, 192.

above, forcing all Japanese to register surnames, was enacted "under pressure from the Ministry of War."[56]

Military concerns were also the prime motivation of the Iranian modernizers, for the first step towards the reestablishment of a centralized state guaranteeing law and order was the creation of a modern conscript army.[57] In the First Majles (legislative assembly, or parliament) (1906–1908), it had been argued that "since the survival of Iran is the duty of every Iranian, young Iranians should perform military service, as is done in other countries."[58] In the Second Majles (1909–1911), the newly established Democrat party advocated for conscription, and a plan was introduced to institute compulsory military service. To counter clerical opposition, this plan was justified by pointing out that this was in accordance with Islam, which mandated that all Muslims were expected to participate in jihad, or holy war. When Prince Farmānfarmā defended the proposal in the parliament, he noted that there was compulsory military service throughout the world but that in Iran, it was not possible just yet because there was no census of the population. There were protracted arguments about this proposal, and it was still pending when the cabinet resigned and parliament was dissolved in 1911 in the wake of the dismissal of Morgan Shuster, as discussed above.[59] Conscription was discussed again in the short-lived Third Majles (1914–1915),[60] and in the years that followed, during World War I, the Iranian state's helplessness to prevent foreign troops from ravaging the country drove home the importance of a standing army. Compulsory military service was high on the agenda of the governments that followed the coup d'état of 1921, and in 1923 Prime Minister Mostowfi al-Mamālek introduced a bill in parliament to institute it. However, conservatives managed to thwart these efforts,[61] and it was therefore only in the Fifth Majles (1924–1926) that a law establishing male conscription was passed – two days after another law had made the registration and adoption of family names obligatory. After much debate, both within and outside the chamber, the ulema obtained the concession that seminarians, muftis, and ulema would be excluded from obligatory military service, provided they passed the requisite examinations. The verification

56. Ibid., 193.

57. For a brief description of Iran's military before the reforms of the 1920s, see Yann Richard, "La fondation d'une armée nationale en Iran," in Yann Richard, ed., *Entre l'Iran et l'Occident* (Paris: Editions de la Maison des Sciences de l'Homme, 1989), 44–49.

58. Moḥammad Vaḥid Qalafi, *Majles va nowsāzi dar Irān (1302-1311 h. sh.)*(Tehran: Nashr-e Ney, 1379/2000), 57–58.

59. Mansoureh Ettehadieh, *The Lion of Persia: a Political Biography of Prince Farmān-Farmā* (Cambridge, MA: Tŷ Aur Press, 2012), 110–111.

60. Qalafi, *Majles va nowsāzi dar Irān*, 63.

61. Cronin, *The Army and the Pahlavi State*, 125–126.

of this process, however, was up to the state, denting the independence of the Shiite clergy.[62] The social power of the latter was also affected by several subsequent measures, as we shall see.

To conclude: in terms of state building, what mattered for Iranian leaders was less the adoption of surnames than the establishment of a centralized civil registry where the personal status of the citizenry was recorded, as this was a necessary precondition for the introduction of general conscription. But it would also improve tax collection: in 1922 the American Arthur Millspaugh had been hired to reorganize Iran's fiscal administration,[63] and soon after the 1925 law was passed, we find his name (along with that of the minister of finance) on a number of circulars (*mottaḥed al-ma'āl*) ordering finance ministry officials in the provinces to do their utmost to help set up the registries and, where they had been set up, to require identity papers from all citizens who called on the local offices of the ministry.[64]

Within the laws establishing state registries, however, those parts that touched on names, along with the law abolishing titles, had their own dynamic and contributed to the transformation of Iranian society. Before we can examine these laws and decrees in detail, we must discuss traditional naming practices, for while these were the very practices targeted by the reformers, they also furnished the raw materials for the new appellations propagated by the state.

62. Qalafi, *Majles va nowsāzi dar Irān*, 122–124.

63. For his own account of his services in Iran, see A. C. Millspaugh, *The American Task in Persia* (New York and London: The Century Co., 1915), 172–286.

64. Vezārat-e māliyeh (Ministry of Finance), edāreh-ye 'āyedāt-e dākheli (Office of Internal Revenues), "Mosā'edat bā ma'murin-e sejell-e aḥvāl" (Assistance to the officials of the Registry Office), 13 Dey 1304 (3 January 1926); Vezārat-e māliyeh (Ministry of Finance), edāreh-ye 'āyedāt-e dākheli (Office of Internal Revenues), "Edāreh-e māliyeh" (Finance Office), Farvardin 1305 (March–April 1926).

2

TRADITIONAL NAMING PRACTICES

NAMES REFLECT SOCIAL STATUS, religious affiliation, ethnicity, moral values, individual characteristics, or, sometimes, coincidental events related to a person.[1] In premodern times, Iranians, like most other peoples, had complicated naming practices for individuals, practices that were far more intricate and variegated than the simple modern two-part appellation consisting of a first and a family name.[2] As the components of traditional Iranian names influenced many Iranians' choice of a family name after 1918, it will be useful to begin by bringing some intelligibility to these vernacular practices.[3] To isolate the elements of an appellation, one convenient place to begin is the structure of names in the classical period of Islamic civilization.

Components of Traditional Iranian Names

A person's name traditionally consisted of five elements: a *kunya* (teknonym, in Persian *konyeh*), an *ism* (proper name, in Persian *esm*), a *nasab* (lineage, patronym), a *nisba* (relational adjective, in Persian *nesbat*), and a *laqab* (title, pl. *alqāb*).[4] Beginning in late medieval times, poets began adding a *takhalluṣ* (pen name, in Persian *takhalloṣ*) to these.[5] It must be noted, however, that "the

1. See Christian Bromberger, "Pour une analyse anthropologique des noms de personnes," *Langages* 66 (June 1982): 103–124.

2. See Richard D. Alford, *Naming and Identity: A Cross-Cultural Study of Personal Naming Practices* (New Haven: HRAF Press, 1987) and the more encyclopedic Eugène Vroonen, *Les Noms des personnes dans le monde: anthroponymie universelle comparée* (Brussels: Éditions de la Librairie Encyclopédique, 1967).

3. These practices also make it difficult for librarians to catalogue books written by Iranians before 1926. See "The Cataloguing of Persian Works: Iranian Personal Names: Their Characteristics and Usage," *Unesco Bulletin for Libraries* 14:5 (September–October 1960): 205–209, 232.

4. This quintipartite classification is taken from Annemarie Schimmel, *Islamic Names* (Edinburgh: Edinburgh University Press, 1989), chapter 1: "The Structure of a 'Name,'" 1–13. A different classification system is used by Garcin de Tassy in his *Mémoire sur les noms propres et les titres musulmans* (Paris: Imprimerie Impériale, 1854). Garcin's treatise is based on a manuscript that he does not identify, however, for which reason I do not engage with his classification.

5. See J.T.P. de Bruijn, "The Name of the Poet in Classical Persian Poetry," in Charles Melville, ed., *Proceedings of the Third European Conference of Iranian Studies*, Part 2: *Mediaeval and Modern Persian Studies* (Wiesbaden: Dr. Ludwig Reichert Verlag, 1999), 45–56.

border between these different types of names [was] very porous."[6] The relevance of these traditional onomastic elements for the creation of surnames can be seen in the fact that among the Persian speakers of Afghanistan, the word *takhalloṣ* came to mean family name,[7] while among the Tajiks of Central Asia it was the word *nasab* that came to signify family name.

The first of these elements, the *kunya*, is a name that designates a person with reference to his or her children.[8] In Arabic it consists of the word *Abu* (father of) or *Umm* (mother [of]) followed by another name, most often a son's proper name. It was introduced to Iran with Islam (e.g., Abu 'Ali Sinā = Avicenna) but largely disappeared after the Middle Ages.[9] However, many male *kunyas* turned into proper names, such as Abolqāsem (Abu al-Qāsem) or Abolḥasan (Abu al Ḥasan).

It is the second of these five elements, proper names—in Persian *esm* or *nām*—that evince the greatest continuity with the present. Although almost all Muslim and even quite a few Jewish Iranians adopted Arabic names following the coming of Islam, the old pre-Islamic Persian names never disappeared. Zoroastrians kept them, and Muslims occasionally carried them as well, to wit Shah Ṭahmāsb (r. 1524–1576), the Safavid dynasty's second (and longest-reigning) monarch. Persian names also reemerged forcefully during the reign of Fatḥ-'Ali Shah Qājār (r. 1797–1834), who gave the names of pre-Islamic kings and heroes to many of his male progeny beginning with his twenty-first son.[10] With the migration of Turks to the Iranian plateau beginning in the eleventh century, Turkish and later Mongol names such as Ṭoghrol and Teymur further enriched Iranians' onomasticon.[11] One peculiarity of Iranian (as well as Arab and Turkish) names to this day is the prevalence of double names for men. These can consist of either two names (Moḥammad 'Ali) or a compound consisting of a name and word, such as

6. D. Penot, *Le Dictionnaire des noms et prénoms arabes* (Lyon: ALIF éditions, 1996), third page of the Introduction (which has no pagination).

7. Thomas Barfied and Omar Sharifi, personal e-mail communications, 29 November 2015 and 8 December 2015, respectively.

8. On teknonymy see Alford, *Naming and Identity*, 90–94.

9. Curiously, it was customary not to mention the *kunya* in the presence of rulers, unless the latter gave their permission to do so. See Iraj Afshār and 'Ali Moḥammad Honar, eds., *Masā'el-e pārisiyeh: Yāddāshthā-ye 'Allāmeh Moḥammad Qazvini*, volume 2 (Tehran: Enteshārāt-e Mowqufāt-e Doktor Maḥmud Afshār, 1390/2011), 32–33.

10. For a full list see Shāhzādeh 'Ażod al-Dowleh, "Solṭān Aḥmad Mirzā," in Doktor 'Abd al-Ḥoseyn Navā'i, ed., *Tārikh-e 'Ażodi* (Tehran: Bābak, 2535/1976), 323–325. Of the shah's sixty sons, sixteen bore Persian or Persianate (e.g. Owrangzib) names. Oddly enough, among the sons of his crown prince, 'Abbās Mirzā, it is the older sons who have Persian names.

11. The borrowing was reciprocal, as shown by the Seljuks of Rum, some of whom bore names such as Kaykhusraw, Kaykaus, and Kayqubad.

'Abd al-Ḥamid, Gholām-Reżā, or Ḥoseyn-Qoli (meaning "slave [of]" Ḥamid, Reżā, and Ḥoseyn, respectively).[12]

The *nasab* expresses a relation to one's ancestors, usually the father. In Arabic this is done by inserting the word *ibn* or *bint* (son or daughter [of]) between the bearer's own name and that of the bearer's father or mother, but in the Persianate world the word *-pur* (son), *-dokht* (daughter), or *-zādeh* (literally "born [of]") can replace *ibn*. Combinations of name + *-dokht* became women's proper names, e.g. Turāndokht.[13] Combinations such as name + *pur* (or *pur-e* + name) or name + *-zādeh* (or *-zād*) were turned into family names when these appeared in the early twentieth century. But in Persian a simple *eżāfeh* (an enclitic *-e*, on which more below) between two names could also denote filiation, as in Rostam-e Farrokhzād, meaning Rostam, son of Farrokhzād.[14]

After the *nasab* comes the *nisba*, a relative adjective that points to one's place of origin, birth, or residence (demonym); indicates one's religious affiliation (especially for non-Muslims); recalls one's profession or trade; establishes one's descent (real or imagined) from a revered person, for instance the Shiite Imams (patronym); or pays homage to an illustrious person or patron. By a happy convergence, the final consonant of the Middle Persian suffix *-ig* (related to Englich *-y*, German *-i[s]ch*, and French *-ique*) was lost (as in English: cf. English *stormy* and German *stürmisch*) in the evolution to New Persian,[15] rendering the New Persian suffix homophonous to the Arabic suffix *-iyy*,[16] which facilitated the adoption of what in Persian is called *yā-ye nesbat* (relative [suffix] *-i*) to form a *nisba*. Because the suffix can be attached to a name, a place, or even a profession, one could have more than

12. In this study double names consisting of two names are written with a space but no hyphen between the two, while those pairing a name with a word that cannot be used as a name by itself are connected by a hyphen.

13. The *kh* was dropped when Carlo Gozzi, Friedrich Schiller, Karl Vollmoeller, and Bertolt Brecht wrote plays titled "Turandot" based on Neẓāmi Ganjavi's Princess Turāndokht, one of the seven princesses in his *Haft Peykar*. Puccini's famous opera *Turandot* is based on Gozzi's version.

14. Nosratollah Rastegar, "Iranische Personennamen neupersischer Überlieferung: Ein Beitrag zu einigen kritischen Werkausgaben klassischer Epen," in Bert G. Fragner, Christa Fragner, Gherardo Gnoli, Roxane Haag-Higuchi, Mauro Maggi, and Paola Orsatti, eds., *Proceedings of the Second European Conference of Iranian Studies* (Rome: Istituto per il Medio Oriente ed Estremo Oriente, 1995), 581–582.

15. It survives in other Iranic dialects/languages, such as Mazandarani, as seen in the pen name chosen by the poet 'Ali Esfandiyāri from the village of Yush, i.e., Nimā Yushij.

16. For a fascinating philological discussion of this convergence see John R. Perry, "New Persian: Expansion, Standardization, and Inclusivity," in Brian Spooner and William L. Hanaway, eds., *Literacy in the Persianate World* (Philadelphia: University of Pennsylvania Press, 2012), 80.

one *nisba*. In the name of the poet Sa'di Shirāzi, for instance, the first *nisba* refers to his patron, the Salghurid ruler of Fars, Atābak Sa'd ibn Zangi, and the second to his home city of Shiraz. It occasionally happened that in some prominent families the same *nisba* would be carried by more than one man, turning it into a *de facto* family name of sorts, even though no one would be addressed by that name.[17] Examples include the Barmaki (Barmecide) family of state administrators in the early 'Abbāsid period and the Majlesi family of clerics in late Safavid times.

Finally, there is the *laqab*, a polysemic term denoting any number of words or phrases used to distinguish one person from others who bear the same name, for which reason the *laqab* can be a greater marker of individuality than a name. The word *laqab* is used very loosely in Iran and can signify informal bynames or nicknames, titles bestowed by a ruler for services rendered to the state, or even honorifics. Bynames can refer to a physical trait, as in Uzun Ḥasan (Ḥasan the tall) or Teymur-e lang (Timur the lame [=Tamerlane]); or a profession, as in 'Omar Khayyām (Omar the tentmaker) or Eskandar Beg Monshi (Eskandar Beg the secretary).

An important category of *laqab*s were the honorary titles bestowed by a ruler (later also by provincial governors) to confer special distinction and dignity on the bearer.[18] These honorary titles usually consisted of two terms, the second of which tended, by the nineteenth century, to be a term connected to the governance of the state, such as *al-Dowleh* (of the dynasty/state, usually used for statesmen), *al-Molk* (of the realm, usually used for literati and functionaries), *al-Mamālek* (of the realms [= Empire]), *al-Salṭaneh* (of the monarchy), or *al-Solṭān* (of the ruler, used for men and women very close to the shah), or else a professional designation such as *al-Aṭebbā'* (physicians), *al-'Olamā'* (clerics),[19] *al-Tojjār* (merchants), or *al-Sho'arā* (poets).[20] For the purposes of this book, I reserve the term "title" for these *laqabs*.[21] In the early Middle Ages this category also included titles ending with *al-Din* ([of] religion) and *-Allāh* ([of] God), but these titles gradually petrified into names, e.g. Shehāb al-Din (Torch of Religion) and Yad Allāh (Hand of God, one of the

17. Rudolf Sellheim, "'Familiennamen' im islamischen Mittelalter," *Orientalia Suecana* 33–35 (1984–1986): 375–384.

18. See *Encyclopaedia of Islam*, new edition, s.v. "laḳab" (by C.E. Bosworth).

19. Apparently Shiite clerics who held a title ending with *al-'Olamā* were known more for their good connections with the state than for their learning. Mirzā Javād Nāṭeq, "Khāṭerāt-e man," manuscript, 32a.

20. Aḥmad Ashraf, "Laqab va 'onvān," in Changiz Pahlavān, ed., *Dar zamineh-ye irānshenāsi* (Tehran: Published by the editor, 1368/1989), 275.

21. Schimmel (*Islamic Names*, 60), perhaps following Garcin de Tassy (*Mémoire*, 6), called these titles *kheṭāb*. According to the standard dictionary of the Persian language, *kheṭāb* means (among other things) "a name or title that contains praise" (*nām va laqab keh dar ān madḥ bāshad*). See *Loghatnāmeh-ye Dehkhodā*, s.v. "kheṭāb," volume 21, 625.

titles of 'Ali ibn Abi Ṭāleb).[22] One exception was *Ẓell Allāh* (Shadow of God), a title occasionally adopted by premodern Iranian rulers and consistently borne by Qājār monarchs, and *Āyat Allāh* (Sign of God, henceforth spelled Ayatollah), which appeared in the early twentieth century as an honorific for high-ranking clerics, perhaps as a counter to the former.[23]

To illustrate this five-part naming matrix, let us take the full name of 'Onṣori (c. 961–c. 1039), the poet laureate of the medieval Ghaznavid court. It was Abu al-Qāsem [*kunya*] Ḥasan [*ism*] ibn Aḥmad [*nasab*] 'Onṣori [his *takhalluṣ*] Balkhi [*nisba* relating him to his place of birth, the city of Balkh]. His *laqab* was Malek al-Sho'arā (King of the Poets).

Of all *laqab*s, only the honorary titles were ever officially abolished, for which reason they deserve to be discussed in greater detail.

Honorary Titles

Honorary titles have a long history in Iran, going back to Achaemenean times. Under the Sasanians, many of the titles bestowed on worthy officials consisted of two elements, for example the word *tahm* (strong) and the name of the monarch.[24] Heribert Busse writes that the memory of these titles combined with the prominence of *laqab*s in the Arabic tradition to yield some of the titles that the 'Abbasid caliphs bestowed, where the Sasanian ruler's name was replaced by the more abstract *al-dawlah* ([of the] state or dynasty, pronounced *dowleh* in modern Iranian Persian). The first to be so honored were viziers, followed by the Hamdanid rulers of Syria and the Buyid rulers of Iraq and western Iran. Of the latter, the brothers 'Ali (r. 934–949), Ḥasan (r. 935–976), and Aḥmad (r. 945–967) were given the titles 'Emād al-Dowleh (Pillar of the State), Rokn al-Dowleh (Column of the State), and Mo'ezz al-Dowleh (Fortifier of the State), respectively,[25] in AD 945, all terms connoting strength.[26]

22. On the latter see Albert Dietrich, "Zu den mit *ad-Dīn* zusammengesetzten islamischen Personennamen," *Zeitschrift der deutschen morgenländischen Gesellschaft* 110:1 (1960): 45–54.

23. Jalāl Matini, "Baḥs̱i darbāreh-ye sābeqeh-ye tārikhi-ye alqāb va 'anāvin-e 'olamā dar maẕhab-e shi'eh," *Irānshenāsi* 1:4 (Summer 1983): 584.

24. Arthur Christensen, *L'Iran sous les Sassanides*, second edition (Copenhagen: Ejnar Munksgaard, 1944), 408–411.

25. These were not the only titles that the Buyid rulers assumed. For detailed discussions see Wilferd Madelung, "The Assumption of the Title Shāhānshāh by the Būyids and 'The Reign of the Daylam (*Dawlat Al-Daylam*)'," *Journal of Near Eastern Studies* 28:2 (April 1969): 84–108; and Lutz Richter-Bernburg, "Amīr-Malik-Shāhānshāh: 'Aḍud ad-Daula's Titulature Re-Examined," *Iran* 18 (1980): 83–102.

26. Heribert Busse, *Chalif und Grosskönig: Die Buyiden im Iraq (945-1055)* (Wiesbaden: Franz Steiner, 1969), 19 and 160. Before Busse, Christensen noted that the Sasanian title *dar-andarzbadh*, "councillor of the court," bore a "singular resemblance" to the title *Moshir al-Dowleh*. Christensen, *L'Iran*, 411.

The conferral of these titles served the dual purpose of exalting the secular rulers, by allowing them indirectly to share the religious and moral influence of the 'Abbasids, and at the same time underlining the caliphs' continued suzerainty over them. The Samanids of Transoxiana did not use such titles for themselves,[27] but did confer them on their Turkish military chiefs—including those who would later oust them and found the Ghaznavid dynasty: Sebüktigin (r. 977–997) and his son Sultan Maḥmud (r. 998–1030), who became Nāṣer al-Dowleh (Helper of the State) and Seyf al-Dowleh (Sword of the State), respectively. Not to be outdone, the caliph bestowed the titles of Yamin al-Dowleh (Right Hand of the State) and Amin al-Milla (Trustee of the People) on Sultan Maḥmud.[28] The Seljuks, who followed the Ghaznavids, carried similar titles and also bestowed them on courtiers, most famously the vizier Neẓām al-Molk (Order of the Realm) and his rival and successor, Tāj al-Molk (Crown of the Realm).

As early as the eleventh century, many were already bemoaning what amounted to an inflation of titles. The polymath Abu Reyḥān Biruni wrote that the pompous titles had become "clumsy to the highest degree, so that he who mentions them gets tired before he has hardly begun, he who writes them loses his time in writing, and he who addresses [people] with them runs the risk of missing the time for prayer."[29] A few decades later, Neẓām al-Molk, the Seljuk grand vizier, complained that:

> There are too many titles, and everything that multiplies loses its power and importance. All kings and caliphs have bestowed titles sparingly, because the dignity of the realm hinges on everybody getting his appropriate title and status. If the title of a man of the bazaar or a peasant is the same as that of a great man, there will be no difference between a plebeian and a noble, and the status of the celebrated and the unknown will be the same.... Thus there was an erudite scholar named Mo'in al-Din [Defender of the Religion] who had a Turkish pupil, also titled Mo'in al-Din, who not only knew nothing about religion, he could not even read or write. Since they had the same title, what is the difference between the scholar and the ignoramus, between judges and servants? This is not right for the country.[30]

27. Navādeh-ye Mohalleb pesar-e Moḥammad pesar-e Shādi, *Mujmal al-tawārīkh wa l'qiṣaṣ*, ed. Seyf al-Din Najmābādi and Zigfrid Veber [Siegfried Weber] (Edingen-Neckarhausen: deux mondes, 2000), 329.

28. C. E. Bosworth, "The Titulature of the Early Ghaznavids," *Oriens* 15 (1962): 210–233.

29. As quoted in Schimmel, *Islamic Names*, 61.

30. Khᵛājeh Neẓām al-Molk Abu 'Ali Ḥasan ibn 'Ali ibn Eshāq Ṭusi, *Siyāsatnāmeh*, ed. 'Abbās Eqbāl (Tehran: Enteshārāt-e Asāṭir, 1372/1993), 185. The fact that the author calls Mo'in al-Din a "name" in the case of the scholar and a "title" in the case of his pupil illustrates the porousness of the borders between names and titles noted above.

Under the rulers of the Safavid dynasty (1501–1722), titles were used sparingly and specifically assigned to certain offices. The grand vizier was titled E'temād al-Dowleh (Reliance of the State), the chief financial official Mostowfi al-Mamālek (Auditor of the Realms), and the controller of the mint Mo'ayyer al-Mamālek (Assayer of the Realms). The *qurchibāshi* (head of the cavalry) was titled Rokn al-Salṭaneh (Pillar of the Monarchy), and the *qullarbāshi* (head of the slave soldiers) Rokn al-Dowleh (Pillar of the State).[31] The founder of the Qājār dynasty (1795–1925), Āghā Moḥammad Khān (r. 1795–1797), resumed the Safavid practice when he gave the title E'temād al-Dowleh to his vizier Ḥājj Ebrāhim Shirāzi, but it was Āghā Moḥammad Khān's nephew and successor Fatḥ-'Ali Shah (r. 1797–1834) who began the practice of "bestowing descriptive titles ending with *al-Dowleh*, *al-Salṭaneh*, *al-Molk*, *al-Moluk*, and *al-Mamālek* not only on high state officials but also on his children, wives, and favorites." At the time an historian predicted that this would lead to an overabundance of titles in the future, and he was to be proven right.[32]

The number of titled subjects further increased under Moḥammad Shah (r. 1834–1848) and in the early years of Nāṣer al-Din Shah's reign (r. 1848–1896). In 1862 Nāṣer al-Din Shah ordered the composition and printing of a detailed memorandum titled *Tashkhiṣ va tarqim-e alqāb*, "The Classification and Recording of Titles." In spite of the publication's name, however, it did not attempt to standardize or fix titulature, instead simply listing the honorofic phrases that had to precede officials' names in letters addressed to them in the name of the sovereign. The short preface states that in their correspondence with each other, people could use whatever formulas they wished (Figure 1).[33]

Nāṣer al-Din Shah ordered his poet laureate, Maḥmud Khān Malek al-Sho'arā Ṣabā, to write another treatise on honorary titles in 1885–1886 (1303 A.H.L.). Only two entries were finished: one on Ṣaḥeb Qerān, the other on Farhād Mirzā Mo'tamed al-Dowleh.[34]

For the fortieth anniversary of Nāṣer al-Din Shah's reign, his minister of publications, E'temād al-Salṭaneh (Reliance of the Monarchy), put together a compendium of miscellaneous information that contains a wealth of information about what contemporaries considered important. Chapter 12 of the document lists all the titles carried by people during the four decades of the Shah's reign up to that point, thus providing an approximation of how many

31. Ashraf, "Laqab va 'onvān": 273.

32. Moḥammad Hāshem Āsaf, Rostam al-Ḥokamā', *Rostam al-tavārikh*, ed. Moḥammad Moshiri (Tehran: Chāp-e Tābān, 1348/1969), 467–471.

33. "Tashkhiṣ va tarqim-e alqāb," *Farhang-e Irānzamin* 19 (1352/1973): 49–61.

34. "Tartib-e alqāb," *Farhang-e Irānzamin* 19 (1352/1973): 62–88.

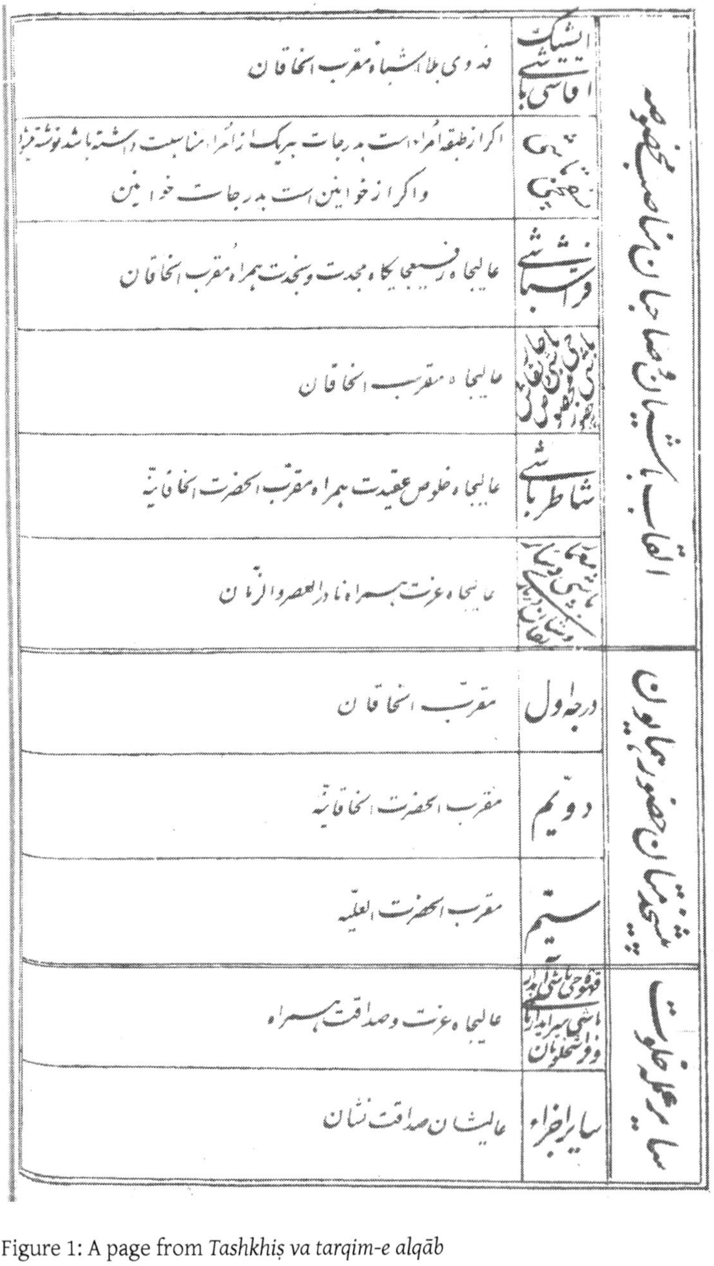

القاب بعضی از صاحب‌منصبان مخصوص	ایشیک آقاسی باشی	فدوی جان‌نثار مقرب الخاقان
	[illegible]	اگر از طبقهٔ امراست بدرجات هریک از امرا مناسبت داشته باشد نوشته شود و اگر از خوانین است بدرجات خوانین
	فراشباشی	عالیجاه رفیع جایگاه مجدت و نجدت همراه مقرب الخاقان
	[illegible]	عالیجاه مقرب الخاقان
	شاطرباشی	عالیجاه خلوص عقیدت همراه مقرب الحضرت الخاقانیه
	[illegible]	عالیجاه عزت همراه نادرالعصر والزمان
پیشخدمتان حضور همایون	درجهٔ اول	مقرب الخاقان
	دویم	مقرب الحضرت الخاقانیه
	سیم	مقرب الحضرت العلیه
سایر عملهٔ خلوت	قهوه‌چی‌باشی [illegible]	عالیجاه عزت و صداقت همراه
	سایر اجزاء	عالیشان صداقت نشان

Figure 1: A page from *Tashkhiṣ va tarqim-e alqāb*

titles were in existence then.[35] It is not an entirely accurate tableau, because the author includes not only titles that were bestowed on individuals to add to their distinction but also job descriptions such as consul or *kārgoẕār* (a state official who dealt with foreign residents) and the professional titles of the heads of certain occupational groups in the employ of the state. The cataloguing of Iranian titles is very far from being an exact science,[36] but the following numbers give an approximation of their distribution in the late 1880s.

Out of a total of 618 entries, a few are atypical in that they lack a second part beginning with the definite article: these include Amir Kabir (Grand Commander), Molk-Ārā (Realm Adorner), and Farmān-Farmā (Order Giver). Of those that include the definite article, three end in *al-Solṭān*, 61 in *al-Salṭaneh*, 75 in *al-Dowleh*, eight in *al-Mamālek*, 71 in *al-Molk*, nine in *al-Vezāreh* ([of the] Ministry), and 18 in *al-Moluk* ([of the] Kings). Some frequent titles point to professions: there are 12 titles ending in *al-Towliyeh* (Administration), these being conferred on administrators of shrines and religious endowments; about 30 titles, most of them ending in *al-'Olamā*, point to clerical incumbents; and about 20, most of them ending in *al-Aṭebbā* ([of the] physicians), designate physicians. A number of these entries do not contain the given name of the carrier; it is highly probable that these refer to women, since it was considered improper to pronounce a woman's name. Most of these female title holders were probably relatives or wives of the shah.[37] These titles without forenames include 30 of the 61 *al-Salṭaneh*s, 20 of the 75 *al-Dowleh*s (most famously Anis al-Dowleh [Companion of the State], Nāṣer al-Din Shah's favorite wife), one of the *al-Molk*s, all 18 of the *al-Moluk*s,[38] and 6 others, giving us probably 75 titled women. Two entries are for eunuchs, namely E'temād al-Ḥaram and Mo'tamed al-Ḥaram, respectively Confidence and Confidant of the Harem. In 1890 another eunuch, Āghā Bahrām, assumed the title Mo'in al-Solṭan (Defender of the Ruler) and signed a telegram with it. When the shah found out, he decreed a morato-

35. Moḥammad Ḥasan Khān, E'temād al-Salṭaneh, *Ketāb al-ma'āẕer va l-āẕār* (Tehran: Dār al-Ṭabā'eh-ye Dowlati, 1306/1927), 230–242.

36. Yann Richard, *Répertoire prosopographique de l'Iran moderne: "Rejâl" (Iran, 1800–1953)* (Paris: Sorbonne Nouvelle, 2012). See 2–4 for the difficulties involved. For a biographical dictionary of Qajar title holders see Mahdi Qominezhād, ed., *Alqāb va manāseb-e 'aṣr-e Qājāri va asnād-e Amin al-Żarb: Yādegāri az Asghar Mahdavi* (Tehran: S̱orayyā, 1388/2009).

37. On women's titles see also Mahasti Abuẕarjomehri, "Alqāb-e zanān dar 'aṣr-e Qājār (bā takkiyeh bar asnād-e Ārshiv-e Melli)," *Faṣlnāmeh-ye Ārshiv-e Melli* 2:2 (Summer 1395/2016): 36–51.

38. Some titles ending in *al-Moluk* became women's forenames, such as the not uncommon Fakhr al-Moluk (Honor of the Kings).

rium on new titles.[39] But when Amin al-Solṭān (Trustee of the Ruler) became prime minister in 1892, a veritable inflation of titles set in, allegedly because the prime minister wished to expand his influence.[40] As ʻEyn al-Salṭaneh (Eye of the Monarchy), one of Nāṣer al-Din Shah's nephews, put it in his diary in 1893:

> They are inventing stranger and stranger titles.... Now we have to use the terms "the first," "the second," and "the third" for some titles, so that [their holders] can be distinguished. For instance, Mo'ayyed al-Salṭaneh the first, Mo'ayyed al-Salṭaneh the second, or Mo'ayyed al-Salṭaneh the third. Or the eastern Mo'ayyed al-Salṭaneh and the western Mo'ayyed al-Salṭaneh, because one is Moḥammad Mehdi Mirzā Hamadāni, the other Mirzā Reżā Khān, the [Persian] minister in Germany. Europe has become the west of Iran! Many titles have become repetitive, such as my fake and pointless title, which three other persons have obtained as well. Now I will have to think of another insipid title for myself.... In no other reign have titles become so debased. Armenians, Jews, and Zoroastrians have titles.[41]

One year later, in 1894, E'temād al-Salṭaneh, the aforementioned minister of publications, noted in his diary that titles were now for sale:[42] "A few months ago the *Kashikchibāshi* [Head of the Sentinels] paid 3,000 tumāns to get the title of Kashikchibāshi for his son and Nāẓem al-Salṭaneh [Regulator of the Monarchy] for himself."[43] This practice went on even within the immediate imperial family:

> Majd al-Dowleh [Glory of the State] has paid 100 ashrafis to get the title Malekeh-ye Irān [Queen of Iran] for his wife, to match the title of Malekeh-ye Jahān [Queen of the World], held by his sister, who is married to the Crown Prince's son. I wish the Shah were aware that Malekeh-ye Irān should be his own wife, and the mother of the crown prince at that.... If [Majd al-Dowleh] wanted a title [for his wife] to match that of his sister, he

39. Moḥammad Ḥasan Khān, E'temād al-Salṭaneh, *Ruznāmeh-ye khāṭerāt-e E'temād al-Salṭaneh*, ed. Iraj Afshār (Tehran: Amir Kabir, 1389/2010), entry for 18 Muḥarram 1308 / 3 September 1890, 987.

40. 'Abd Allāh Mostowfi, *Sharḥ-e zendegāni-ye man*, volume 1 (Tehran: Ketābforushi-ye Moḥammad 'Ali Foroughi, 1324/1945), 588–589.

41. Qahramān Mirzā Sālur, 'Eyn al-Salṭaneh, *Ruznāmeh-ye khāṭerāt-e 'Eyn al-Salṭaneh (Qahramān Mirzā)*, ed. Mas'ud Sālur and Iraj Afshār, volume 1 (Tehran: Asāṭir, 1374/1995), 560.

42. This practice was not unknown in Europe, either. Under Prime Minister David Lloyd George the sale of titles of nobility reached such proportions that the British Parliament in 1925 passed an "Honours (Prevention of Abuses) Act" that made the sale of peerages and other honors illegal. See Andrew Cook, *Cash for Honours: The True Life of Andrew Gregory* (Stroud: History Press, 2008).

43. E'temād al-Salṭaneh, *Ruznāmeh-ye khāṭerāt*, entry for 27 Jumādā II 1312 / 26 December 1894, 987.

> should have taken Malekeh-ye Zamān [Queen of the Age]. Of course these titles, such as Malekeh-ye Jahān Khānom and Malekeh-Irān Khānom, are [in actuality] like names. On the whole, titles lack any dignity and respect. I fear that people will gradually become so impertinent that they will take the title of Pādeshāh-e Irān [King of Iran] for themselves. So take heed O men of sight! [Koran 59:2].[44]

The government repeatedly announced that it would put an end to the unchecked proliferation of titles, but after every official announcement to this effect there would be a relapse to the indiscriminate granting of *laqabs*,[45] mostly to men but occasionally to women as well.[46] Even foreign residents of Tehran were honored: around 1892 Nāṣer al-Din Shah's Swedish dentist, Bertrand Hybennet, received the very apposite title Mosannen al-Salṭaneh, "Dentist of the Monarchy."[47] By then titles had become hereditary occasionally, to the point where a brother of a court poet titled Shams al-Sho'arā (Sun of the Poets) inherited that title upon the poet's death even though he was not a poet himself.[48] According to one acerbic critic of the system, good-looking young courtiers received two-part titles beginning with *shokuh* (glory) or *mesbāḥ* (lamp), or ending with *khalvat* (intimacy), while members of the lower ranks of the state administration received titles ending in *divān*.[49] There was also an increase in military-sounding titles that included words such as *sardār* (commander), leading 'Eyn al-Salṭaneh to observe that "with one or two exceptions these *sardārs* have never seen a naked blade or a drawn sword. Their noses have never smelled the smoke of gunpowder. Besides, these irregular and incompetent troops do not need that many officers."[50]

Title inflation, it is worth noting, was (like the sale of titles) not unknown elsewhere. In France, the reign of Louis XIII saw such an increase,[51] and on the eve of the French Revolution, one observer wrote: "Aujourd'hui ... les titres d'honneur [sont] usurpés de la manière la plus scandaleuse."[52]

The conferral of titles was still a somewhat formal affair under Nāṣer

44. Ibid., 24 Jumādā II 1312 / 23 December 1894, 987.

45. Sālur, *Ruznāmeh*, volume 1, 581, 634–635, 627, and 851.

46. Ibid., 635, 678, 697, and 793.

47. Ibid., 635. For more on Hybennet see "The Swedish Dentist of the Shah," *New York Times*, 8 May 1896.

48. E'temād al-Salṭaneh, *Ruznāmeh-ye khāṭerāt*, entry for 11 Dhu l'Qa 'da 1309 / 7 June 1992, 816.

49. Nāṭeq, "Khāṭerāt-e man," 32b.

50. Sālur, *Ruznāmeh*, volume 1, 883. See also Aḥmad Majd al-Eslām Kermāni, "Kharid va forush-e manāṣeb va alqāb dar Irān," *Yād* 18 (1382/2003): 310.

51. Dominique de la Barre de Raillicourt, *Les titres authentiques de la noblesse en France* (Paris: Perrin, 2004), 32–39.

52. Antoine Maugard, *Remarques sur la noblesse: dédiées aux assemblés provinciales* (Paris: Chez Lamy et Gattey, 1788), 3.

al-Din Shah, and for each title a firman was issued, the recipient of the title showing his gratitude by offering between fifty and hundred gold coins to the imperial treasury. (This practice was largely discontinued under Moẓaffar al-Din Shah [r. 1896–1907], however, when a simple written note [*dastkhaṭṭ*] issued by a secretary took the place of the firman.) The modernist politician Yaḥyā Dowlatābādi reported that in late Qājār times the granting of titles had become a source of income for a number of people: the man who wrote out the firman, the one who took it to the Shah for his approval, the one who put the imperial seal on it, the one who put the prime minister's seal on it, and the one who devised the *ṭoghrā* (calligraphic monogram, used for seals and official documents) for the bearer of the new title.[53] Titles ending with *Solṭan*, hitherto reserved for men close to the Shah, became widespread.[54] In principle, honorary titles were bestowed on individuals only, but in practice a son sometimes inherited his father's title, such as the statesman Hasan Pirniyā, who upon his father's death was given the latter's title of Moshir al-Dowleh (Councilor of the State).[55] The same person could thus hold different titles at different stages in his or her life.

Towards the end of the dynasty, some people just started assuming titles, which their relatives and friends used to address them with, until the person eventually became publicly known by that title.[56] Alternatively, a man would write a letter of congratulations to the Court, signing it with the title he had adopted, and when a reply arrived addressing him with that title, he would take that to mean that his title had been bestowed by the Sovereign.[57] Titles were also given by provincial authorities: the governors of Tabriz and Urmia thus gave titles to Assyrian physicians who had graduated from a medical school that had been founded by American missionaries in Urmia.[58]

53. Yaḥyā Dowlatābādi, *Tārikh-e ʻaṣr-e ḥāżer yā Ḥayāt-e Yaḥyā*, volume 4 (Tehran: Ebn-e Sinā, 1331/1952), 397.

54. Qahramān Mirzā Sālur, ʻEyn al-Salṭaneh, *Ruznāmeh-ye khāṭerāt-e ʻEyn al-Salṭaneh (Qahramān Mirzā)*, ed. Masʻud Sālur and Iraj Afshār, volume 2 (Tehran: Asāṭir, 1376/1997), 1115.

55. Iraj Afshār, "Shesh Moshir al-Dowleh," *Bokhārā* 75 (Farvardin-Tir 1389 / March–June 2010): 552. This article was first published in *Jahān-e Now* in 1326 (1947). On the title Moshir al-Dowleh, which was also carried by men unrelated to the Pirniyā family see Mahdi Najjāri, *Chegunegi-ye eʻtā-ye alqāb-e moshābeh dar dowreh-ye Qājār (Motāleʻeh-ye mowredi bar ru-ye laqab-e Moshir al-Dowleh)* (Tehran: Nedā-ye Tārikh, 1394/2015), 51–123.

56. Mostowfi, *Sharḥ-e zendegāni-ye man*, volume 1, 587–592.

57. Ashraf, "Laqab va ʻonvān": 278–279; Majd al-Eslām Kermāni, "Kharid va forush": 312–313.

58. Hānibāl Gevergiz, *Tārikhcheh-ye dāneshkadeh-ye pezeshki-ye Orumiyeh* (Tehran: Enteshārāt-e Dāneshgāh-e ʻOlum-e Pezeshki-ye Tehrān, n.d.), 112. I thank Eden Naby for making this book available to me.

It is interesting to note that Qājār shahs bestowed the title *prans* (prince) on four state officials, namely Mirzā Malkam Khān Nāẓem al-Dowleh (Regulator of the State), Mirzā Esḥāq Khān Mofakhkham al-Dowleh (Illustrious of the State), Mirzā Reżā Khān Arfa' al-Dowleh (Highest of the State), and Moḥammad 'Ali 'Alā' al-Salṭaneh (Notable of the Monarchy).[59] As a rank of nobility (rather than the designation of a member of a ruling house), "prince" (*Fürst* in German) is not common in Western Europe, and its adoption by the Iranian Court was probably inspired by the Russian rank of *knyaz* (a cognate of *king* and *König*), traditionally carried by a number of aristocratic families but also occasionally bestowed by the czars on individuals and customarily translated as "prince."[60] The introduction of the title of "prince" in Iran, proudly used by its carriers in Europe,[61] was likely a timid attempt at acculturation to the practice of European rulers, analogous to the introduction of the *kazoku*, a hereditary nobility patterned on the British peerage, by the Meiji reformers in Japan in 1884.[62]

Outside Iran, grandiose honorary titles were particularly popular in India,[63] where they had spread in the wake of the conquest of eastern Iran and northern India by the Ghaznavids.[64] Even the British awarded them occasionally: it is ironic that a number of Parsi priests in India, for example, received the Arabic title *Shams ul-Ulama* (Sun of the Clerics) from the British.[65] These titles survived at the courts of Muslim rulers until the end; among the many titles borne by the last Nizam of Hyderabad, a state forcefully incorporated into the Indian Union in "Operation Polo" in 1948, were (to use the official orthography) Muzaffar-ul-Mulk-Wal-Mamalik, Nizam ul-Mulk, and Nizam ud-Daula.

59. Bāqer 'Āqeli, *Ruzshomār-e tārikh-e Irān az mashruṭeh tā enqelāb-e eslāmi* (Tehran: Nashr-e Goftār, 1369/1990), 91 n1.

60. Peter the Great granted it to his associate Alexander Prince Menshikov, and Catherine the Great to her lover Grigory Potemkin.

61. Notice, for instance, a book published by Arfa': Le Prince Mirza Riza Khan Daniche Arfa-od-Dovleh, *Poésie et Art Persans à Monaco* (Monte Carlo: Imprimerie du "Petit Monégasque", 1919). Arfa' al-Dowleh later took the surname Arfa'.

62. The *kazoku* was abolished in 1948. See Takie Sugiyama Lebra, *Above the Clouds: Status Culture of the Modern Japanese Nobility* (Berkeley: University of California Press, 1993), 51–61.

63. Cf. the dialogues of the fictitious Indian Kamāl al-Dowleh and Iranian Jalāl al-Dowleh in the writings of the modernist intellectuals Mirzā Fatḥ-'Ali Ākhundzādeh and Mirzā Āqā Khān Kermāni.

64. See for instance Mohammad Yusuf Siddiq, *Epigraphy and Islamic Culture: Inscriptions of the Early Muslim Rulers of Bengal (1205–1494)* (New York: Routledge Taylor & Francis, 2016), chapter 4: "Diversity of Titles in the Islamic Inscriptions of Bengal," 69–109.

65. Monica M. Ringer, *Pious Citizens: Reforming Zoroastrianism in India and Iran* (Syracuse: Syracuse University Press, 2011), 116, 119, 127.

Naming Practices in the Early Twentieth Century

In addition to the five constituents of a name discussed above, a number of other terms could frame the given name of an Iranian, adding to the possibilities for individuation. On the eve of the Constitutional Revolution, the situation was as follows:

Literate men put a *Mirzā* before their name (e.g. Mirzā Reżā Kermāni, the assassin of Nāṣer al-Din Shah); if placed after a name, *Mirzā* indicated descent from a shah (e.g. the poet Iraj Mirzā).[66] Upper-class men, especially members of landowning families and tribal chieftains, added *Khān* or *Beyk* to their names (but the title of *Khān* could also be bestowed by the shah). Merchants and ulema, meanwhile, preferred the word *Āqā* for the purpose of adding distinction. Similar terms used by women were *Khānom*, *Bibi*, and *Begum*.[67] Combinations of these terms were also possible, such as in Mirzā Āqā Khān Kermāni, the modernist intellectual whose proper forename, 'Abd al-Ḥoseyn, was displaced by a triad of terms none of which is an actual name. The name of a master craftsman might be preceded by *Ostād* (Master, often shortened to *Us* or *Ustā*). A champion athlete or strong man might have his name preceded by the word *Pahlavān* (hero, wrestler). A number of other additions had to do with religion: *Mollā*, *Ākhund*, *Mojtahed*, and *Sheykh* designated men of religious learning, the last one commonly used for Shiite clerics who did not claim descent from the Prophet. *Darvish* and *Pir* signaled a Sufi; *Seyyed* and *Mir* signified descent from the Prophet through his daughter Fatima. *Ḥājj(i)* indicated that the bearer had accomplished the pilgrimage to Mecca (or Jerusalem, in the case of Jews). Those Shiites who could not afford the pilgrimage to Mecca might still want to indicate that they had visited the tombs of the third Imam in Karbala or the eighth Imam in Mashhad, by putting a *Karbalā'i* (sometimes shortened to *Kal*) or a *Mashhadi* (usually contracted to *Mash*, *Masht*, or *Mashti*) before their given name.[68] This allowed for individuation even among siblings: in his memoirs, the merchant Ḥājj

66. On the two meanings of Mirzā and the linguistic principles explaining the positioning of the word, see John R. Perry, "*Mīrzā*, *Mashtī* and *Jūja Kabāb*: Some Cases of Anomalous Noun Phrase Word Order in Persian," in Charles Melville, ed., *History and Literature in Iran: Persian and Islamic Studies in Honour of P.W. Avery* (London: British Academic Press, Cambridge University, 1990), 213–228.

67. These terms can be compared to the Spanish *don* and *doña*.

68. This summary obviously reflects Iran's majority Twelver-Shiite population. For a good study of how a similar dynamic plays out in a Sunni Persian (and Uzbek) environment, see Pierre Centlivres, "Noms, surnoms et termes d'adresse dans le nord afghan," *Studia Iranica* 1:1 (1972): 89–102. Descendants of the Caliph Abu Bakr, for instance, bear the hereditary honorific *Khᵛājah*, and those of the Caliph 'Omar that of *Ṣāḥebzādah*.

Moḥammad Taqi Jurābchi, for instance, lists his brothers as Mashhadi Naqi, Karbalā'i (Moḥammad) Bāqer, Mashhadi Shafi', and Ḥājj Reżā.[69]

In addition to the various elements of a person's name, there was another set of words that was used when referring to or addressing a person politely, whether orally or in writing, including *jenāb* (proximity or refuge, implying that the person so addressed provided protection), *ḥażrat*, *ḥożur* (both meaning presence), and *khedmat* (service). These honorifics, called *'onvān* (pl. *'anāvin*) in Persian, were markers of respect and at time bestowed by the ruler personally,[70] and their use could easily slide into flattery, if not outright sycophancy.[71] Around the middle of the nineteenth century, the honorific *Ḥojjat al-Eslām* (Proof of Islam) began to be used for a few top clerics, and around the time of the Constitutional Revolution, as mentioned earlier, the honorofic *Āyat Allāh* (Sign of God) appeared for leading mujtahids.[72]

The various components, both onomastic and honorific, and the order in which they appeared were scrupulously respected when speaking of a person, leading the German diplomat Wilhelm Litten to remark that an Iranian's name could easily be deciphered: "Ḥajji Mirzā Reżā Khān is an educated Iranian named Reżā who had the means to go to Mecca." He contrasted this with the situation in the Ottoman Empire, where it was "a special science to find one's way among the many Mukhtar Pashas and Mukhtar Beys."[73] But not all foreigners found Iranian naming practices as transparent as did Litten, a trained Orientalist. W. Morgan Shuster, the hapless treasurer-general of Iran in 1911, found Iran's system of names and titles "absurdly complicated": "Imagine a gentleman in American political life deciding that he would adopt and wear the title of 'Marshal of the Marshals,' or 'Unique One of the Kingdom,' or 'Fortune of the State.' ... It is rather difficult for foreigners to remember these appellations."[74]

69. Ali Gheissari, "Merchants without borders: Trade, Travel and a Revolution in Late Qajar Iran (the Memoirs of Hajj Mohammad-Taqi Jourabchi, 1907–1911)," in Roxane Farmanfarmaian, ed., *War and Peace in Qajar Persia: Implications Past and Present* (London: Routledge, 2008), 188.

70. The shah's Franco-Mauritian physician Joseph-Désiré Tholozan, for instance, was officially granted the *'onvan jenāb*. See Moḥammad Ḥasan Khān, E'temād al-Salṭaneh, *Ruznāmeh-ye khāṭerāt-e E'temād al-Salṭaneh*, ed. Iraj Afshār (Tehran: Amir Kabir, 1389/2010), entry for 16 Muḥarram 1299 / 8 December 1881, 135.

71. Ashraf, "Laqab va 'onvān": 283–299.

72. Matini, "Baḥs̱i darbāreh-ye sābeqeh-ye tārikhi-ye alqāb": 560–608.

73. Wilhelm Litten, "Persische Familiennamen," *Der Neue Orient* 6:5 (1920): 196. In fact, the use of titles such as Pasha and Bey was highly regulated and standardized in the Ottoman Empire. See Dr. Stephan Kekule, *Über Titel, Ämter, Rangstufen und Anreden in der offiziellen osmanischen Sprache* (Halle: Druck und Verlag von C.A. Kaemmeren & Co., 1892).

74. W. Morgan Shuster, *The Strangling of Persia* (1912, Washington, DC: Mage, 1987), xvi.

Just as hereditary second names had appeared in Europe centuries before their use was formalized, and in Japan many rich farmers and townspeople carried them before the Meiji Restoration and in spite of their official prohibition under the Tokugawa shogunate[75] (exceptions could be made for artists and master craftsmen[76]), in Iran, too, a few Iranians adopted family names in the late nineteenth century, decades before the state required citizens to do so. As with so many cultural innovations in Iran and other countries like it, the adoption of family names was occasioned by external stimuli. By the later nineteenth century, elite Iranians were regularly visiting Europe, where they were expected by the authorities to present a surname. Upper-class Iranians who enjoyed sustained contact with Europe therefore began adopting family names. Litten tells us of the above-mentioned Mirzā Reżā Khān Mo'ayyed al-Salṭaneh (Supporter of the Monarchy), who in Berlin adopted the name Gerānmāyeh (Of Precious Content), which the Germans promptly bowdlerized to "Kranmayer." Another Iranian resident of Germany, Esmā'il Beg (Beyk), married a German woman in the 1880s; the registrar turned them into Mr. and Mrs. Beck.[77] Conversely, Europeans who moved to Iran permanently often Persianized their surnames. Thus the Frenchman Jules Richard, who introduced many innovations to the Court, converted to Islam, and became an Iranian subject, passed the surname Rishār to his progeny.[78]

The numerous Iranian merchants engaged with trade in the Russian empire often added an *-ov* to a personal name or a *-ski* to their place of origin to create a surname on the Russian model,[79] such as Kāshānski, for instance, the name of a family whose roots lay in the city of Kāshān and who traded in Ashgabat, across the border from Iran in what is today Turkmenistan. Given the Russian influence in northern Iran and the capitulatory rights Russian subjects enjoyed in Iran, some Iranian subjects placed themselves under Russian protection in order to gain immunity from Iranian courts. Aḥmad Matin-Daftari, who would later become minister of justice and, briefly, prime minister, wrote in his doctoral dissertation:

75. Herbert Plutschow, *Japan's Name Culture: The Significance of Names in a Religious, Political and Social Context* (Sandgate: Japan Library, 1995), 169–180.

76. Inge-Lore Kluge, "Die heutigen japanischen Familiennamen und ihre Entstehung in historischer Sicht," in Rudolf Schützeichel and Alfred Wendehorst, eds., *Erlanger Familiennamen-Colloquium: Referate des 7. interdisziplinären Colloquiums des Zentralinstituts* (Neustadt an der Aisch: Degener, 1985), 121–128.

77. Litten, "Persische Familiennamen": 197.

78. *Encylopaedia Iranica*, s.v. "Rishār Khān" (by Shireen Mahdavi).

79. For an analysis of Russian surnames and their derivation from patronyms see Joseph Schütz, "Russische Familiennamen," in Schützeichel and Wendehorst, eds., *Erlanger Familiennamen-Colloquium*, 41–47.

> Under whatever pretext, the Russian legation allowed itself to present as Russian protégés Persian citizens whose birth and familial ties left no shadow of a doubt about their Persian origin. These protected persons, enjoying consular jurisdiction to the detriment of their compatriots, would become docile slaves of Russian diplomacy. In their capacity as merchants or large landowners, they could exercise great influence in the country in favor of their masters. They encouraged other Persians to follow their example. Gradually, every malevolent Persian who wanted to oppress his neighbor, kill an opponent with impunity, usurp the inheritance of a minor, refuse to pay his taxes, etc., had only to add an "ov" in the Russian manner to his Persian name, for instance Aliov, to solicit Russian protection. A large landowner who did not want to put himself directly under Russian protection so as not to lose his political rights, such as his access to the council of ministers and to parliament, could simply employ a tenant who had Russian nationality or protection in order to annex all the lands neighboring his village.[80]

In the aftermath of the Constitutional Revolution, surnames ending with *-zādeh* seem to have been particularly popular, especially in Azerbaijan, e.g. Seyyed Ḥasan Taqizādeh.[81] This trend came to Iran from the Caucasus and the Ottoman Empire, where the Persian ending was used alongside the Turkish ending *-oğlu*. In fact, the use of the ending *-zādeh* had a long history beyond the borders of Iran. In Ottoman practice, a patronym formed on the model of [name] + *-zade* often preceded a person's forename; in Ottoman Albania, Evliya Çelebi tells us, "most of the names are like Cemalizade, Kasımzade, etc."[82]

80. Dr. Ahmad Khan Matine-Daftary, *La suppression des capitulations en Perse: L'ancien régime et le statut actuel des étrangers dans l'Empire du "Lion et Soleil"* (Paris: Presses universitaires de France, 1930), 81. See also Bābā Safari, *Ardabil dar goẕargāh-e tārikh*, volume 2 (Ardabil: Islamic Azad University Press, 1991), 8.

81. Qahramān Mirzā Sālur, 'Eyn al-Salṭaneh, *Ruznāmeh-ye khāṭerāt-e 'Eyn al-Salṭaneh (Qahramān Mirzā)*, ed. Mas'ud Sālur and Iraj Afshār, volume 8 (Tehran: Asāṭir, 1379/2000), 6541; N. A. Belgorodskii, "Sotsial'nyi element v persidskikh imenakh, prozvishchakh, titulakh i familiiakh," in *Zapiski Instituta Vostokovedeniia Akademii Nauk*, volume 1 (Leningrad: Izdatel'stvo Akademii Nauk SSSR, 1932), 222–223.

82. Robert Dankoff and Robert Elsie, ed. and trans., *Evliya Çelebi in Albania and Adjacent Regions (Kosovo, Montenegro, Ohrid)* (Leiden: Brill, 2000), 179.

3

THE MODERN STATE STEPS IN

TRADITIONALLY, IRAN HAD NO SYSTEM OF FORMAL REGISTRIES. Muslims recorded births and the newborn's given name in the family Koran or a prayer book,[1] Jews did the same in the Torah,[2] and Baha'is used the *Ketāb-e Aqdas* for that purpose.[3] Deaths were marked on tombstones; marriages and divorces were recorded by each religion's officials. It was not until after the end of World War I that the Iranian state began centralizing these functions.

The Law of 1918 and Its Aftermath

On 12 September 1918 (20 Sonboleh [Mehr] 1297), the Iranian cabinet approved a law establishing a Personal Status Registry (the country had no sitting parliament at the time), and it would appear that the minister who pushed for it the most was Firuz Mirzā Noṣrat al-Dowleh (Victory of the State), the minister of justice. The law was termed *Qānun-e Sejell-e Aḥvāl*, meaning literally "law of the recording of situations."[4] It was signed by the following cabinet members: Vos̱uq al-Dowleh (the prime minister), Firuz Mirzā, 'Ali-Qoli, Moshār al-Molk, Naṣir al-Dowleh, and Dabir al-Molk.[5] The fact that in signing the law, Firuz Mirzā chose to omit his title of Noṣrat al-Dowleh is itself indicative of the importance he attached to the law.

The law was published in the semiofficial newspaper *Irān* on 9 October, to go into effect on 14 October of that year.[6] Article 3 asked every family head to choose a surname for himself and his relatives, while Article 4 specified the information that had to be included in the identity document: surname,

1. Moḥammad Ḥejāzi, "Āmār va s̱abt-e aḥvāl," in *Mihan-e mā* (Tehran: Enteshārāt-e Vezārat-e Farhang, 1338/1959), 611.
2. Homa Sarshar, personal e-mail communication, 8 November 2015.
3. Mehrdad Amanat, personal e-mail communication, 8 November 2015.
4. At least one observer found this terminology ridiculous, since he could not see that it had anything to do with names, birth dates, parents, or children. Moḥammad Javād Morādiniyā, ed., *Ruznāmeh-ye khāṭerāt-e Seyyed Moḥammad Kamareh'i*, volume 2, *moqaddamāt-e kudetā-ye sevvom-e Esfand* (Tehran: Shirāzeh, 1382/2003), 1207. The date of the entry is Monday 16 Ṣafar 1338 / 10 November 1919.
5. *Irān*, 16 Mizān [Mehr] 1297 / 9 October 1918, 2.
6. *Irān*, 20 Mizān [Mehr] 1297 / 13 October 1918, 1.

name(s), title, place of birth, date of birth, name of the father, and name of the mother. Article 5 defined a person's name as consisting of a surname, first name, and the demonym of the place where he or she was born and where his or her birth had been registered, the example given being Eskandar Sāsān Tehrāni. Article 6 noted that titles were conferred by the state and could be recorded in the registry either before or after the name, as might be appropriate. To be registered, the document conferring the title had to be verified by the registrar. Article 32 said that family heads had to go to the registry office in person and register the personal status of all those family members who were still under their authority or lived in their house.

But for that to happen, of course, registry offices had to be set up.[7] According to Article 8, an office would be set up in every town, and Article 9 specified that in localities where functioning police commissariats existed, these would house the registries, while in their absence district governors or village headmen would be responsible for registering the details of people's personal status. Article 39 laid down that the law would have immediate effect in Tehran but that elsewhere it would be implemented at opportune moments (a reflection of the fact that, as we saw in chapter 1, much of the country was not effectively controlled by the central state). The life events to be registered in the identity papers were birth, death, marriage, and divorce, and the clergy were assigned the task of forwarding marriage and divorce certificates to the registries (Articles 23–26). Article 31 specified that the dates be given in the solar *Jalāli* (solar Hijri) calendar, which had become Iran's official calendar in 1911,[8] although it was permissible to add the date according to the *qamari* (lunar Hijri) calendar. Article 36 brought home the importance of the new identity papers by establishing that they had to be presented in order to obtain documents such as voting cards, passports, or gun licenses.

The benefits of the new law were apparently not clear to everyone, for they were explained in an editorial published in *Irān* two months later. The article began by asserting that a country that had been devoid of any kind of useful legislation of the sort that is necessary for the development of a national life and institutions, a country deprived until now of laws that would

7. Over the years these offices were placed under the authority of different state institutions. For details see Doktor Ḥoseyn Maḥbubi Ardakāni, *Tārikh-e mo'assesāt-e tamaddoni-ye jadid dar Irān*, volume 2 (Tehran: Mo'asseseh-ye Enteshārāt va Chap-e Dāneshgāh-e Tehrān, 1376/1998), 157–161.

8. In the *Jalāli*, or Solar Hijri, calendar, the months correspond to the signs of the zodiac. Like the Lunar Hijri calendar, it begins with the migration (*ḥijra*) of the Prophet Muhammad from Mecca to Medina in AD 621. It was made official in Afghanistan in 1922. See *Encyclopaedia Iranica*, s.v. "calendars."

bring it "closer to civilization," would perhaps not immediately recognize the benefits of such a law. In the long run, the article explained, the new law would make it possible to have population statistics, one of the most vital necessities for a nation. But there were benefits in the short run as well: most families, especially middle-class families, had had no family names until now, which meant that after two generations they forgot about their ancestors. Now that names and titles were registered, all kinds of fraud in matters such as marriage and commercial contracts would be preventable. No one would be able to obtain false papers to claim to be the subject of a foreign power and thus make a nuisance of himself. The mere fact that every family would adopt a surname for itself, and that a forename and a family name would suffice to identify people, "just as was the case in civilized countries," would put an end to one of the social ills that plagued Iran, namely the adoption of empty titles, because one of the reasons that titles had been so popular in Iran was the absence until now of family names that rendered individuals distinguishable. Another benefit was that the judiciary would spend less time on cases of fraud, as no transaction would henceforth be valid unless the parties were properly identified by their papers; no one would be able to sell someone else's lands by fraudulently adopting his identity. Finally, the article averred that the nationhood of a people could not be assured in the absence of the kind of information that would henceforth be gathered by the registry offices, for a state had to know its citizens in order to distinguish them from foreigners.[9] The same issue of *Irān* ran an advertisement in which, probably *pour encourager les autres*, the commissioner for Tehran's ninth district (the city's 'Udlājān quarter), Seyyed Moṣṭafā Khān, and his deputy, 'Isā Khān, announced that they had adopted the surnames Rāsekh Qā'em Maqāmi and Pishruyān, respectively (Figure 2).[10]

Iranian men were now free to choose surnames for their families, but some thought that others were not choosing wisely. In late December 1918, the poet laureate, Moḥammad Taqi Bahār, who had chosen his pen name (*takhalloṣ*) as his surname, published an editorial in which he asserted that personal "tastes, suggestions, and wishes" were the factors determining the choice of surnames. He reminded his readers that names contained no truth or effect in and of themselves, adding:

> The goodness or badness of a name is nothing but an illusion. The letters and rhymes of a name contain no effect; Arabic, Persian, Turkish, and

9. *Irān*, 17 Qows [Āẕar], 1297 / 9 December 1918, 1.

10. Ibid., 2. It is interesting to note that neither of the two followed the instructions contained in Article 5 of the law specifying that a name had to contain the demonym corresponding to one's birthplace.

> French words have no bearing on the effect of a name. It is only the education a family head gives his family that will render that name grand, influential, and famous. Some, thinking that fame lies in names, choose the names of famous and illustrious people for themselves!

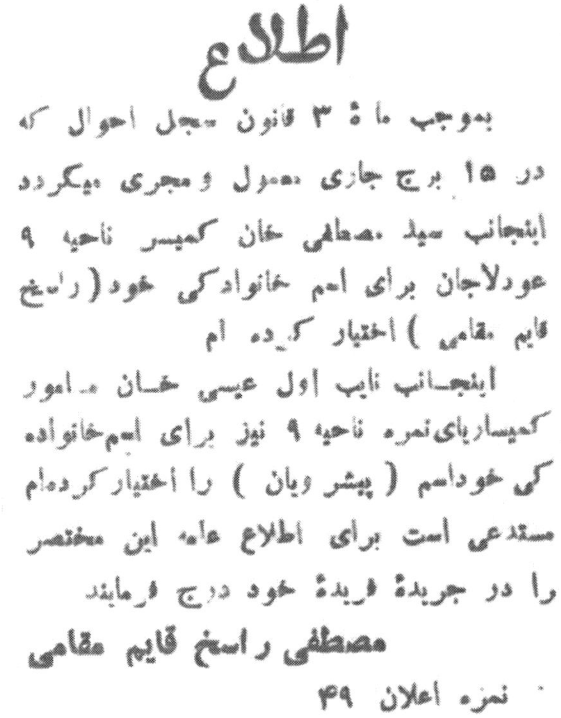

اطلاع

بموجب ماده ۳ قانون سجل احوال که
در ۱۵ برج جاری معمول و مجری میگردد
اینجانب سید مصطفی خان کمیسر ناحیه ۹
عودلاجان برای اسم خانوادگی خود (راسخ
قایم مقامی) اختیار کرده ام
اینجانب نایب اول عیسی خان مامور
کمیساریای نمره ناحیه ۹ نیز برای اسم خانواده
گی خود اسم (پیشرویان) را اختیار کرده ام
مستدعی است برای اطلاع عامه این مختصر
را در جریده فریده خود درج فرمایند

مصطفی راسخ قایم مقامی

نمره اعلان ۳۹

Figure 2: Announcement of family names

While conceding that everyone was free to choose a family name, to wit a man who had adopted the surname Johudkhor (Jew eater), he advised his readers not to adopt names (of famous poets) like Ferdowsi, Manuchehri, or Sa'di.[11] Bahār's admonition seems to have had little effect, however, for in a diary entry for January 1919, the aforecited Prince 'Eyn al-Salṭaneh, by now also a grand-uncle of the reigning Shah, wrote:

> Noṣrat al-Dowleh insists on family names.... People have to go to a commissariat and choose a family name for themselves. Since in Iran and

11. *Irān*, 1 Jodey [Dey] 1297 / 23 December 1918, 1.

in the Persian language there are few names, and since, unlike in Europe, people do not choose rare and unusual names, people are constantly arguing about family names, even in the newspapers. Some new families and races have appeared on the scene that nobody had heard of until now. One says he is of the race of Sāsān, the other descends from the Kiyān, yet another becomes a Saljuq.[12] His neighbor is a descendant of Ashkbus, Giv, Gudarz,[13] you name it. Everybody wants to attach himself to an important person and adopt that clan's or person's [name]. They even assail Iran's poets and wise men and call themselves Ferdowsi, Farrokhi, Sa'di etc. and claim to be of their race.[14]

In 1919, newspapers began carrying notices in which men informed the public of the family name they had chosen. Disregarding Bahār's advice like others already mentioned, a cleric from Qom linked himself to the Koran and called himself Forqāni, after the sura *al-furqān*, justifying his choice with a poem: (Figure 3)[15]

نام خانواده

چون من غریب بودم وازقرآن غریب تر

این نام خانواده گیرم گشت اختیار

یاران و دوستان بشناسند زین سپس

فرقانی است نام من از روی افتخار -

ملا محمد فرقانی قمی وحسن فرقانی قمی

نمره اعلان ۳۷۳

Figure 3: A rhymed announcement

12. The names of three Persian dynasties.
13. The names of three heroes from the *Shāhnāmeh*.
14. Qahramān Mirzā Sālur, 'Eyn al-Salṭaneh, *Ruznāmeh-ye khāṭerāt-e 'Eyn al-Salṭaneh (Qahramān Mirzā)*, ed. Mas'ud Sālur and Iraj Afshār, volume 7 (Tehran: Asāṭir, 1378/1999), 5504–5505.
15. *Irān*, 24 Jodey [Dey] 1297 / 15 January 1919, 1. "Forqān," literally "a criterion for separating right and wrong," connotes the Koran here.

Since I was a stranger and find awe in the Koran
I have chosen Forqāni for a family name.
My friends shall know this from now on:
Forqāni is the name I am proud to claim.

In February 1919 an advertisement appeared in *Irān* that seemed to suggest that the inhabitants of Tehran were showing insufficient alacrity in going to the registry. It warned that if people did not adopt a surname, not only would their descendants make fun of them thirty years in the future but all chic, refined, and appropriate names would have been taken and the procrastinators would, like Europeans, be reduced to adopting the names of birds, animals, insects, and plants. As a public service, the newspaper set up a help desk that offered to create "modish, chic, and appropriate" surnames for those who had no time to think of one. All they had to do was to send the editorial offices a letter containing their family relations and their own tastes and inclinations, and within twenty-four hours they would be given a euphonious name the announcement of which, whether in prose or in verse, would attract positive attention (Figure 4).[16]

قانون سجل احوال — میز مساعدت

همه بخوانید

قانون سجل احوال – بهترین قوانین اجتماعی که در ایران وضع شده است ، ساده ترین ضروریات عمومی که فواید آن در حال حاضر معلوم نائبه رسید بالیه – مطابق اخلاق عمومی ، دیانات و آداب ملی ، این قانون نقض نمی‌شود ، ولازم الاجری است کسانی که در ثبت اسم خانوادهٔ خود اهمال میکنند ، سال دیگر مطابق قانون مجازات خواهند شد ، وسی سال دیگر اولاد انها باانها خندیده وانها را بکهنه پرستی و لاقیدی بالجاج منسوب خواهند داشت .

بشتابید ، ونام خانوادهٔ خود را در دفاتر سجل احوال قید نمائید – ورنه اسامی شیک وظریف ومناسب اتمام شده و مجبورید مثل اروپا اسامی طیور یا سایر حشرات وحیوانات و نباتات را انتخاب کنید .

ادارهٔ ایران برای انتخاب اسامی شیک مجانا حاضر است کسانی که اسم مد و شیک ومناسب میخواهند ، و خود مجال تهیه وانتخاب انرا ندارند ، ملاحظات خانوادگی خود را با ذوق و تمایلات خویش را با آدرس خود باداره ایران فرستاده خود پس از یک شبانه روز مطالبه جواب کنند ، اسم های ثبت نشده وقشنگ وبا حشمت لفظی که بخواهند ، با عبارات خوش اسلوب که اعلان آن قابل توجه گردد – چه نظما و چه نثرا – برایشان تهیه خواهد شد ، یا اگر خود اسمی تهیه کرده اند ، ادارهٔ ما اعلان انها را چه نظما وچه نثرا تهیه خواهد کرد .

میز مخصوصی دراداره برای این خدمت عمومی تدارک شده ونام آن میز (مساعدت) است – اطلاعات را هم بهمان میز میتوان داده قبض رسید گرفت .

(دفتر ایران)

Figure 4: Modish, chic, and appropriate names

16. *Irān*, 24 Dalv [Bahman] 1297 / 13 February 1919, 1.

One such euphonious name was Bāvand, which was adopted by three men who claimed descent from the Sasanians through one Bāv b. Shāpur b. Kayus b. Qobād, founder of the Bāvand dynasty of Mazandaran (Figure 5).[17]

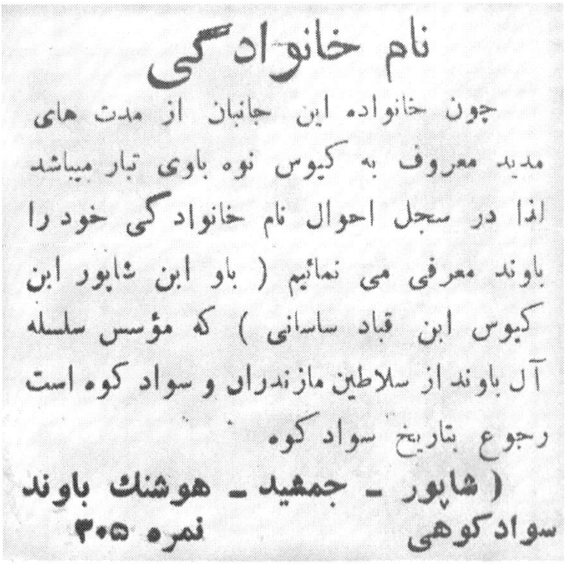

نام خانوادگی

چون خانواده این جانبان از مدت های
مدید معروف به کیوس نوه باوی تبار میباشد
لذا در سجل احوال نام خانوادگی خود را
باوند معرفی می نمائیم (باو ابن شاپور ابن
کیوس ابن قباد ساسانی) که مؤسس سلسله
آل باوند از سلاطین مازندران و سواد کوه است
رجوع بتاریخ سواد کوه

(شاپور ـ جمشید ـ هوشنگ باوند
سوادکوهی نمره ۳۰۵

Figure 5: Distinguished ancestors

Two brothers whose uncle, a certain Ḥājj Ḥoseyn Khān Sālār Manṣur, had chosen the surname Manṣur, chose to call themselves Manṣuri, a very traditional way of establishing affiliation with a revered person through a *nisba* (see chapter 2). Meanwhile, a man whose father, Mo'tamen Lashkar (Trustee of the Army), had been martyred in Tabriz by unscrupulous people because of his innate honesty, called himself Shahidi, *shahid* meaning "martyr." (Figure 6)[18]

On 28 February 1919 the cabinet issued a decree that as of 7 December (15 Qows [Āẕar]) of that year, all state officials would be required to ask for the identity papers of residents of Tehran when carrying out their official duties. If a patron had no identity card, the official should refuse to serve him. In another decree, the cabinet amended the Personal Status Law to specify more precisely the duties of the clerics who administered marriages and divorces to convey the information to the registry.[19]

17. *Ra'd*, 9 Ḥut [Esfand] 1297 / 28 February 1919, 2. See *Encyclopaedia Iranica*, s.v. "Āl-e Bāvand" (by Wilferd Madelung).
18. *Ra'd*, 9 Ḥut [Esfand] 1297 / 28 February 1919, 4.
19. Ibid., 1 and *Ra'd*, 9 Ḥut [Esfand] / 28 February 1919, 1.

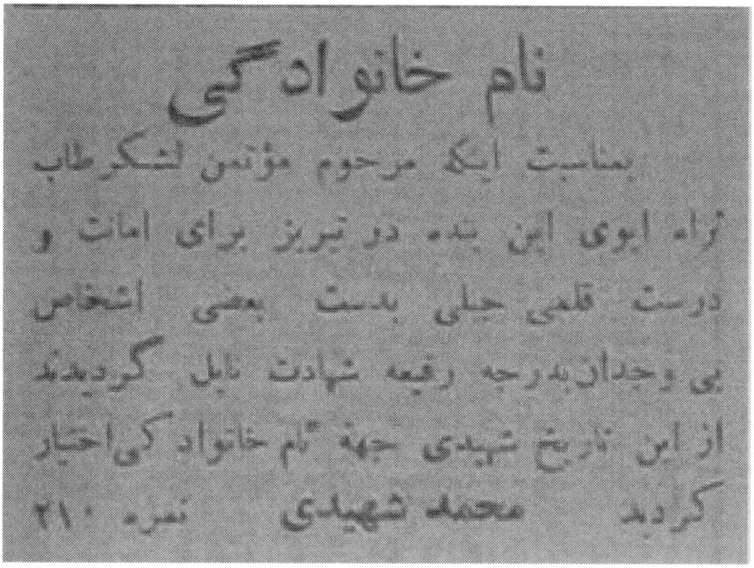

نام خانوادگی

بمناسبت اینکه مرحوم مؤتمن لشکر طاب
ثراه ابوی این بنده در تبریز برای امانت و
درستقلمی خیلی بدست بعضی اشخاص
بی وجدان بدرجه رفیعه شهادت نائل گردیدند
از این تاریخ شهیدی جهة نام خانوادگی اختیار
گردید محمد شهیدی نمره ۲۱۰

Figure 6: Martyrdom

One who immediately saw the ramifications of the state's new role was Wilhelm Litten, who wrote:

> From the viewpoint of a philologist, this measure is noteworthy: the most imaginative nation has to come up with names! The philologist of the future who studies the etymology of names will have to remember the year 1919!
>
> But even from the point of view of constitutional law this measure is remarkable. Formally, it should be noted that until now the authentication of personal transactions, such as marriages, was in the hands of the clergy. This principle has been abolished: apparently it is secular offices that now maintain these registers. Moreover, it is only with this measure that major reforms become possible in Persia: conscription and income tax were unrealizable dreams until now in a country of whose inhabitants only a few carry titles and the remaining ten million share a dozen forenames.[20]

There was some popular resistance to the measures. As 'Eyn al-Salṭaneh noted in January, "they insisted that women be taken to the commissariat, but the clergy and people protested, so that now first-class princes, the clergy, and women are exempted from having to appear at the commissariat [in person] and someone else can represent them."[21] Clerical opposition was addressed in an article published in *Irān* in March. The author, most

20. Wilhelm Litten, "Persische Familiennamen," *Der Neue Orient* 6:5 (1920): 198.
21. Sālur, *Ruznāmeh*, volume 7, 5504–5505.

probably a cleric himself, first justified the new institution by pointing out that, since the Prophet Muḥammad had banned the hoarding of wealth, as a consequence of which Muslims had to receive their income from the public treasury (*beyt al-māl*), the second caliph had instituted an office where Muslims registered their names and those of their dependents and received their income in proportion to the numbers of each household. His successor 'Ali ibn Abi Ṭāleb had maintained this institution, which proved that there was nothing un-Islamic about the new civil registry. The other objection, that one could not expect a man to reveal his wife's name to an agent of the state, the writer dismissed as a false conception of honor whose baselessness was demonstrated by the fact that when a man married or divorced his wife, he had to reveal her name anyway. Moreover, the new law had many benefits: it made it impossible for Ḥasan to collect five state salaries under five different names, and it would be easier to conduct a census, which was vital in times of hardship when victuals had to be rationed. In conclusion, the author asked the government to make it easier for individuals to declare who they were by relieving them of the duty to bring along two witnesses, which was difficult to arrange. He also asked that high-ranking clerics be exempted from having to go to the registry. Instead, officials should be sent to the clerics' homes to register their personal status.[22]

The postwar years were an unsettling time in Iran, however, and the state infrastructure only had a weak presence across the country, such that most people remained unaware of the duty to adopt a surname. Moreover, it seems to have been a more or less voluntary matter at first. One man who did register a surname was a general of the Cossack Division by the name of Reżā. On 3 November 1919 (11 'Aqrab [Ābān] 1298) he asked for identity papers, registering his family name as Pahlavi. The conventional wisdom that Reżā Shah chose the name Pahlavi for his "dynasty" would therefore seem to be inaccurate, since there is little indication that at the time he registered, more than a year before carrying out the coup d'état that brought him to power, he was thinking of founding one. (Figure 7)[23] In 1921, the civil registry was put under the authority of the municipality of Tehran, but because the means available for its implementation were insufficient, that implementation remained limited.[24]

22. *Irān*, 26 Ḥut [Esfand] 1297 / 17 March 1919, 2. The article is signed by one Nur al-Din Kermānshāhāni Āl-e Āqā.

23. http://www.titreemroz.ir/fa/news/15189/%D8%B4%D9%86%D8%A7%D8%B3%D9%86%D8%A7%D9%85%D9%87-%D8%B1%D8%B6%D8%A7%D8%B4%D8%A7%D9%87-%D8%B1%D8%A7-%D8%A8%D8%A8%DB%8C%D9%86%DB%8C%D8%AF-%D8%AA%D8%B5%D9%88%DB%8C%D8%B1. Accessed on 20 July 2017.

24. Qalafi, *Majles va nowsāzi dar Irān*, 126.

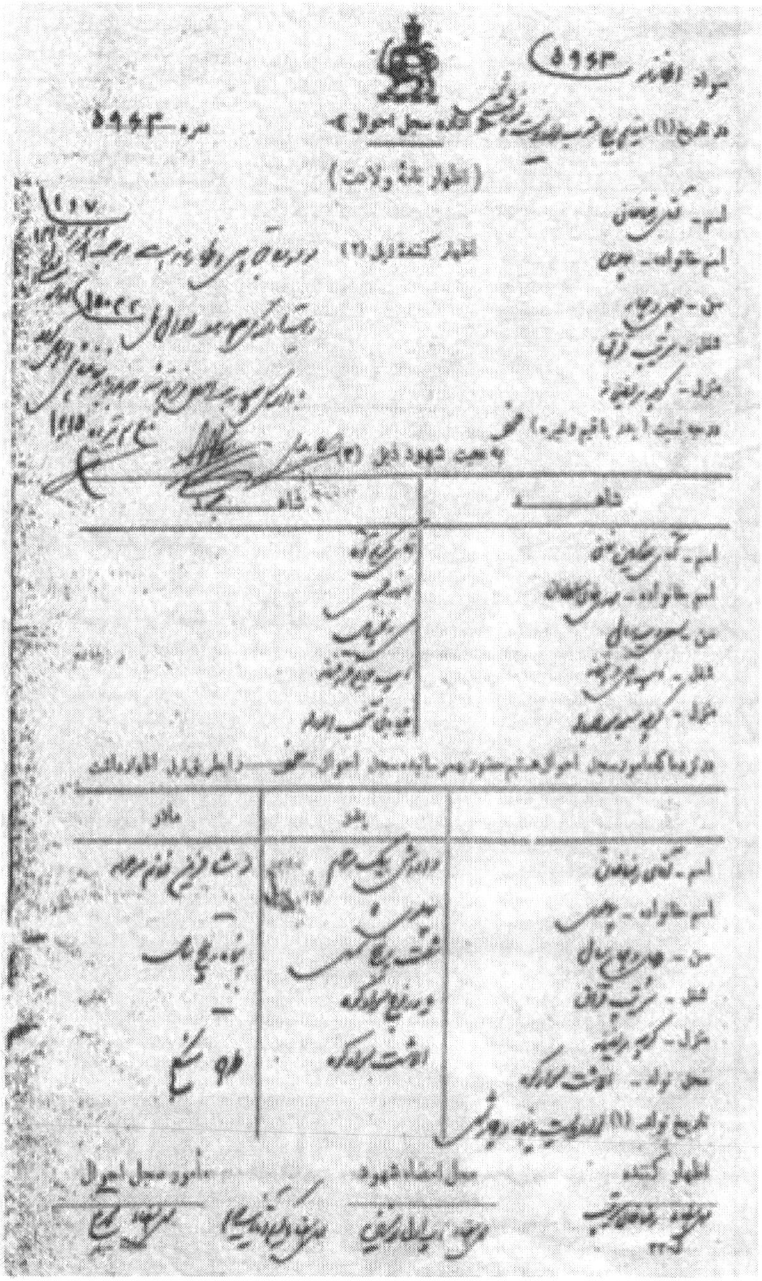

Figure 7: Reza Pahlavi's birth certificate

Soon the honorifics used in both oral and written communication came under attack. In 1921 *Irān* carried the following announcement, whose argumentation is reminiscent of Biruni's complaint, quoted above, about clumsy, pompous titles:

Fighting Shameful Customs

> The Iranian has become used to talking more than is necessary and paying greater attention to fancy titles (*alqāb*) and honorifics (*'anāvin*) than to spiritual [matters]. Modernists, who believe in the simple, unadorned truth, have expressed their fatigue with and hatred for the propagation of these honorifics and titles and their desire for the abolition of these verbal excrescences which cause loss of time and create many problems in correspondence. The *Irān* newspaper wants to put this reform into practice and proposes this measure to all modernists. Anyone who is willing to write only the word *Āqā* on envelopes instead of all those useless honorifics should inform the editorial office, and his name will be printed in a column under the title "Abolition of Honorifics" that will appear on page four of the newspaper.... The printing fee to have one's name included is the minimal sum of five shāhis.[25]

Notices began to appear. In one titled *Elghā-ye 'ādāt-e shum* (The Abolition of Shameful Customs), a number of men stated: "We, the undersigned, ask our friends and acquaintances to desist from writing any honorifics (*'anāvin*) before our names and to content themselves with Āqā."[26] A few weeks later, a Mirzā Asad Allāh Khān Showkat al-Solṭān (Magnificence of the Ruler) informed the public that he wished to be known by the name of Mojarrad. (Figure 8)[27]

In subsequent years, the number of notices announcing new family names diminished, perhaps because any men in the capital who were likely to adopt one had already done so.[28] But as more people adopted family names, conflicts occurred over family names that had been adopted by more than one person. As early as 1919, the newspaper *Ra'd* carried notices in which people demanded that others who had adopted the same name as

25. Quoted in Qahramān Mirzā Sālur, 'Eyn al-Salṭaneh, *Ruznāmeh-ye khāṭerāt-e 'Eyn al-Salṭaneh (Qahramān Mirzā)*, ed. Mas'ud Sālur and Iraj Afshār, volume 8 (Tehran: Asāṭir, 1379/2000), 6125.

26. *Irān*, 1 Asad [Mordād] 1300 / 24 July 1921, 4.

27. *Irān*, 26 Asad [Mordād] 1300 / 18 August 1921, 4.

28. For a parody of what a conversation among modernists might sound like see Sālur and Afshār, eds., *Ruznāmeh*, volume 8, 6541.

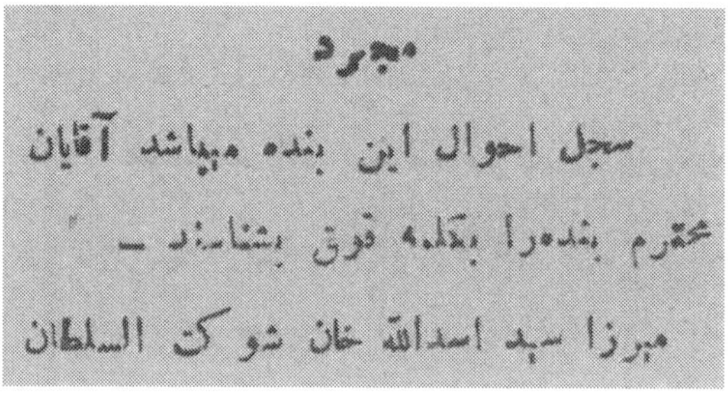
مجرد
سجل احوال این بنده میباشد آقایان
محترم بنده‌را بکلمه قرق بشناسند ـ
میرزا سید اسدالله خان شوکت السلطان

Figure 8: New name, signed with title

they had find a new name for themselves.[29] And sometimes people did: a Dr. Seyyed Nur Allāh, who announced on 13 October 1921 (20 Mizān [Mehr] 1300) that he had chosen Ṣeḥḥat (Health) as his family name, retracted it a fortnight later because "there had been opposition," chosing Mo'ālej (Healer/ Attending [Physician]) instead.[30] This process went on for a few years. In early 1924 we find a notice titled "Warning" (*tazakkor*), stating (Figure 9):

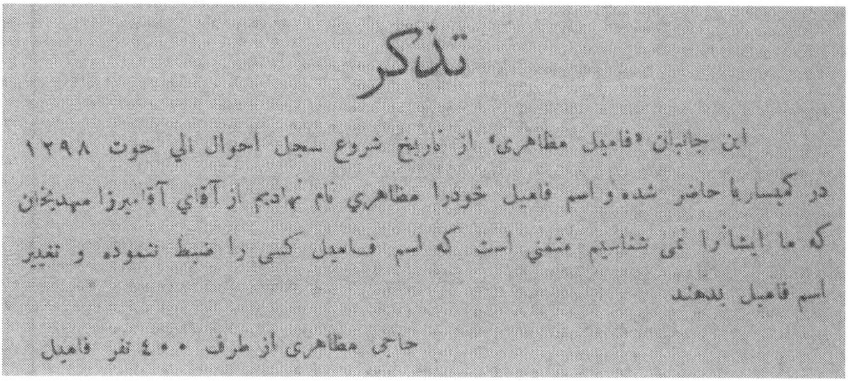
تذکر
این جانبان «فامیل مظاهری» از تاریخ شروع سجل احوال الی حوت ۱۲۹۸
در کمپانیا حاضر شده و اسم فامیل خودرا مظاهری نام نهادیم از آقای آقا میرزا مهدیخان
که ما ایشانرا نمی شناسیم متمنی است که اسم فامیل کسی را ضبط ننموده و تغییر
اسم فامیل بدهند
حاجی مظاهری از طرف ۴۰۰ نفر فامیل

Figure 9: Don't steal other people's surnames

> We, the Maẓāheri family, have been present at the Registry Office from the introduction of *sejell-e aḥvāl* until Ḥut 1297 (March 1919) and adopted Maẓāheri as our family name. We ask Mirzā Mehdi Khān, whom we do not know, not to take other people's names and adopt a new one.
>
> Ḥājji Maẓāheri on behalf of 400 relatives.[31]

29. Litten, "Persische Familiennamen: 197.
30. *Irān* 20 Mizān [Mehr] 1300 / 13 October 1921, 4 and *Irān* 9 'Aqrab [Ābān] 1300 / 1 November, 4, respectively.
31. *Irān*, 26 Dalv [Bahman] 1302 / 15 February 1924, 4.

The notices were occasionally a little puzzling. In 1925 we find a somewhat cryptic notice saying: "My family name is Moḥammadi, and my telephone address is the same. [Signed:] Gholām-'Ali Moḥammadi." (Figure 10)[32]

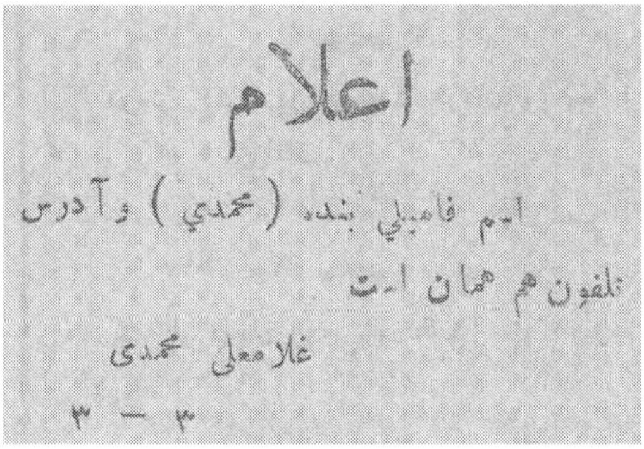
اعلام

اسم فامیلی بنده (محمدی) و آدرس
تلفون هم همان است
غلامعلی محمدی
۳ — ۳

Figure 10: Name and telephone connection

As for titles, they still remained the privilege of the elite; the average peasant, nomad, or city dweller had to be content with one name, and perhaps a nickname to distinguish him from others with the same name. The establishment of constitutional government did not abolish the grandiose titles and honorifics of the elite, and their bearers continued using them. It was this elite character of the honorary titles that created opposition to them in the wake of the Constitutional Revolution of 1906.

After the coup d'état of 1921, which had been accompanied by populist gestures, poets and journalists began making fun of the inflation of titles, but old habits died hard. "Reżā," as he signed his communiqués, was honored with the title Sardār Sepah (Commander of the Army) by Aḥmad Shah immediately after the coup,[33] and in late summer of 1921 the official newspaper *Irān* was still carrying notices that titles had been bestowed on worthy men by the ruler.[34] In 1922, the cabinet issued a decree standardizing a hierarchy of honorifics for high state officials.[35]

32. *Irān*, 24 Jodey [Dey] 1303 / 14 January 1925, 1. The man was probably referring to the address he used for person-to-person calls.

33. Bāqer 'Āqeli, *Ruzshomār-e tārikh-e Irān az mashruṭeh tā enqelāb-e eslāmi* (Tehran: Nashr-e Goftār, 1369/1990), 101.

34. *Irān*, 13 Sonboleh [Shahrivar] 1300 / 5 September 1921, 1, where Āqā Mirzā Seyyed 'Abd Allāh Khān becomes Motarjem al-Molk (Interpreter of the Realm), and *Irān*, 29 Sonboleh [Shahrivar] 1300 / 21 September 1921, 2, where Āqā Mirzā Moḥammad Ḥasan Ardabili becomes Shams al-Ḥokamā (Sun of Physicians), the initiative for the latter having come from the Ministry of Health.

35. Sālur, *Ruznāmeh*, volume 8, 6672.

Increasingly, these titles were parodied. By the autumn of 1923, there were two clowns in Tehran known as Shaghāl al-Dowleh (Jackal of the State) and Babr al-Salṭaneh (Tiger of the Monarchy).[36] The writer Ḥasan Moqaddam, who became famous for parodying superficially Europeanized Iranians in his play *Ja'far Khān az Farang bargashteh* (Master Ja'far Has Returned from Europe), poked fun at titles in his play *Irāni Bāzi* (Acting Like an Iranian), where the action takes place in the year 2000: in that play, Iranians have become so Europeanized that ministers bear titles such as *Conserve* al-Mamālek (Jam of the Realms), *Ecrevisse* al-Salṭaneh (Shrimp of the Monarchy), *Salade* al-Shari'eh (Salad of the Sharia), and *Pantoufle* al-Ḥokamā (Slipper of the Wise/Physicians).[37]

Even outside Iran the bombastic titles of Persian officials invited parody. In 1923, a novel titled *Le Chah du Mahboulistan: Histoire Orientale* was published pseudonymously in Paris.[38] Its premise is that one of Fatḥ-'Ali Shah's sons, named Ḥoseyn 'Ali Bayrām Mirzā, has rebelled and created a small kingdom for himself on the southeastern frontier of Iran, which he calls Māhbolestān. As explained in the book, the name derives from *māh* (moon) and *bolbol* (nightingale),[39] but it is in fact a bilingual pun, for in French *maboule* means "somewhat mad," and in Persian *mahbol* means "vagina." Early on, we read that upon crowning himself, the king auctioned off titles, bestowing those of *Cerveau des Empires* (Maghz al-Mamālek?), *Sabre de la Royauté* (Seyf al-Salṭaneh?), and *Géomètre des Empires* (Mohandes al-Mamālek?) on his prime minister, minister of war, and minister of public works, respectively.[40] The plot of the novel revolves around the state visit to France of the then king of Māhbolestān and is a parody of the visits of the Qājār shahs. The author of this novel was Jacques de Morgan, a French archaeologist who in 1912 had been dismissed from his position as head of the French archaeological delegation to Iran, which had enjoyed a monopoly on digs in Iran since 1900.[41] (The idea of the statelet Māhbolestān was, incidentally, less fanciful than it might seem, for in the nineteenth century the

36. Iraj Afshār, ed., *Nāmehhā-ye Pāris az Moḥammad-e Qazvini beh Seyyed Ḥoseyn-e Taqizādeh* (Tehran: Nashr-e Qaṭreh, 1384/2005), 93.

37. Vaḥid Ayubi, ed., *Zendegi va gozideh-ye āsār-e Ḥasan-e Moqaddam* (Tehran: Ketābsarā-ye Nik, 1385/2006), 68.

38. Karagueuz Effendi, *Le Chah du Mahboulistan: Histoire Orientale* (Paris: "Le Livre", 1923). *Karagöz* is the wily peasant in the traditional Ottoman shadow plays that bear his name.

39. Ibid., 3.

40. Ibid., 5.

41. Nader Nasiri-Moghaddam, *L'archéologie française en Perse et les antiquités nationales (1884-1914)* (Paris: Éditions Connaissances et Savoirs, 2004), 192–193.

British had played with the idea of creating one ruled by Ḥasan 'Ali Mirzā Shojā' al-Salṭaneh [Courageous of the Monarchy], a son of Fatḥ-'Ali Shah, in Herat and Iranian Khorasan.[42])

By 1923, mocking titles had become part of the repertoire of the anti-Qājār campaign being waged by those who advocated the establishment of a republic on the model of neighboring Turkey, where the House of Osman had lost its throne (but not yet the caliphate) in November 1922. In his entries for the year 1923, the indefatigable diarist 'Eyn al-Salṭaneh notes a poem that had appeared in the press linking titles to the dynasty:

> Bas keh laqab ze har ṭaraf gofteh shod o shenideh shod
> Dowleh o molk o Salṭaneh bar sar-e har seh r...eh shod
> Har laqab-e qolombeh'i, chon torshi-ye anbeh'i
> Yā keh cho gusht o donbeh'i bā samani kharideh shod.
> ...
> Bi jahati o bi sabab dādeh shodeh ānqadr laqab
> Tā keh beh qowl-e Kal Rajab shireh-ye ān keshideh shod.
> Bachcheh-ye Mashdi Mamdali chort zadeh ze tanbali
> Gashteh negun ze ṣandali, ru-ye zamin lamideh shod.
>
> So many titles are uttered and heard all the world long
> That *dowleh*, *molk*, and *Salṭaneh* have been sh.. upon.
> Every highfalutin' title, like mango pickle
> Or like meat and sheep fat, is bought for a song.
> ...
> Without rhyme or reason so many titles have been given
> That, as Kal Rajab says, their virility's gone wrong
> Mashdi Mamdali's son is so lazy he's gone to sleep
> Fallen from his chair, he is on the ground, sidelong.[43]

(Mashdi Mamdali was a nickname for Moḥammad 'Ali Shah; his son was the reigning Aḥmad Shah, the end of whose rule was now in sight.)

The Laws of 1925–1928

On 3 Ābān 1302 / 25 October 1923, the leader of the February 1921 coup, Reżā Khān, was named prime minister. Only four days later, on 29 October, a republic was declared in Turkey, and when on 2 November Aḥmad Shah left for Europe, ostensibly for health reasons, the fate of Iran's monarchy seemed to

42. For details see Homā Nāṭeq, *Irān dar rāhyābi-ye farhangi 1834–1848* (London: Payām, 1988), 83.

43. Qahramān Mirzā Sālur, 'Eyn al-Salṭaneh, *Ruznāmeh-ye khāṭerāt-e 'Eyn al-Salṭaneh (Qahramān Mirzā)*, ed. Mas'ud Sālur and Iraj Afshār Ma'ud Sālur and Iraj Afshār, volume 9 (Tehran: Asāṭir, 1379/2000), 6776.

be sealed as well. Elections were held for the Fifth Majles, and the prime minister used his control of the military to ensure that he came first in all electoral districts and that candidates sympathetic to him won seats. Parliament convened on 22 Bahman 1302 / 11 February 1924.[44] Modernist statesmen such as Seyyed Ḥasan Taqizādeh, Malek al-Sho'arā Bahār, Moṣaddeq al-Salṭaneh, the Pirniyā brothers, and Z̲okā' al-Molk (Acumen of the Realm) Forughi were elected and proceeded to sit as independents. Also elected were a small group of oppositionists headed by the cleric Ḥasan Modarres. Reżā Khān's immediate supporters were Western-oriented reformers such as 'Ali Akbar Dāvar and Seyyed Moḥammad Birjandi (Tadayyon), who had not been statesmen under the late Qājārs and who formed the Tajaddod (Revival) party, which held about forty seats. These deputies took the lead in passing state-building and nation-building legislation during the Fifth Majles.[45] Together with the fourteen socialists led by the Qājār prince Soleymān Mirzā, they set out to follow the Turkish example and declare a republic, with Reżā Khān as president.[46] Many Tajaddod deputies were newspaper editors, and the press campaign against the Qājārs intensified: the year 1924 saw what Iranian historiography calls the "republican fever." According to Yaḥyā Dowlatābādi, Reżā Khān essentially wanted three things from the Fifth Majles: an increase in the budget of the military to about half of the total government budget, the establishment of general conscription, and to be named shah. This shows, again, that the reform of Iranian naming practices was closely linked to the introduction of conscription.

According to the published diary of Soleymān Behbudi, the private secretary of Reżā Khān/Shah, sometime in mid-March 1924 the then prime minister received a letter in an envelope on which his name was written, preceded and followed by a string of honorifics so long that a second line was needed: *Ḥożur-e mehr-ẓohur-e bandegān-e ḥażrat-e mostaṭāb-e ajall-e akram-e ashraf-e amna'-e a'ẓam-e āqā-ye Reżā Khān Sardār Sepah vazir-e jang va ra'is al-vozarā' va farmāndeh-ye koll-e qovā' dāmat 'aẓamatoh* (which translates as "to

44. Yaḥyā Dowlatābādi, *Tārikh-e 'aṣr-e ḥāżer yā jeld-e chehārom-e Ḥayāt-e Yaḥyā* (Tehran: Ebn-e Sinā, 1331/1952), 304.

45. This legislation included such measures as the adoption of the metric system and the enactment of a commercial code, a trademark law, and, most importantly, a public penal code, which was instituted in stages.

46. See Ervand Abrahamian, *Iran Between Two Revolutions* (Princeton: Princeton University Press, 1982), 120–135; Cyrus Ghani, *Iran and the Rise of Reza Shah: From Qajar Collapse to Pahlavi Rule* (London: I.B. Tauris, 1998), 289–324; Ḥoseyn Makki, *Tārikh-e bist-sāleh-ye Irān*, volume 2, *Moqaddamāt-e taghyir-e salṭanat* (Tehran: Nashr-e Nāsher, 1362/1983), 413–586, and volume 3, *Enqerāż-e Qājāriyeh va tashkil-e selseleh-ye diktātori-ye Pahlavi* (Tehran: Nashr-e Nāsher, 1382/1983); and Zahrā Shaji'i, *Nokhbegān-e siyāsi-ye Irān az enqelāb-e mashruṭiyat tā enqelāb-e eslāmi*, volume 3, *Hey'at-e vazirān-e Irān dar 'aṣr-e mashruṭiyat* (Tehran: Enteshārāt-e Sokhan, 1372/1993), 146–148.

the attention of the affection-revealing slaves of the excellent presence of the most praised, most generous, most noble, most exalted, most grand Mr. Reżā Khān, general of the army, minister of war, prime minister, and commander-in-chief, may his grandeur last"). Reżā Khān thereupon summoned 'Adl al-Molk (Justice of the Realm), the deputy prime minister, and told him that he wished for all honorifics thenceforth to be dropped on letters addressed to him. On the same occasion, he renounced his title of Sardār Sepah and asked to be addressed as Reżā Khān Pahlavi,[47] using the surname he had registered in 1919. In early April of that year (1924), he told visitors that, unlike people elsewhere in the world, Iranians do not like their names. Soon thereafter, the ministries received instructions to refer to him either as prime minister (*ra'is al-vozarā*) or as Reżā Pahlavi.[48]

When Seyyed Ḥasan Modarres, the leader of the Majles minority, which opposed the republican idea (and therefore also Reżā Khān's dictatorship), was slapped in the face by a Revival party deputy, this assault on the personal dignity of a leading cleric led to anti-republican demonstrations on 3 Farvardin 1304 / 23 March 1925. Reżā Khān was personally involved in the violent repression of the demonstrations.[49] To mend his relations with the clergy afterwards, the prime minister went to Qom, and upon his return to the capital, on 1 April, issued a communiqué in which he renounced the idea of establishing a republic.[50] The ultimate goal of ousting the Qājārs was not abandoned, however, and the press continued its agitation against the hapless Aḥmad Shah and his brother, Crown Prince Moḥammad Ḥasan Mirzā, who was the regent in Tehran while the shah was in France. Finally, in late 1925, Reżā Khān had the parliament vote to topple the dynasty; he himself assumed the crown a few weeks later. In the meantime, the government turned its attention to legislation. This included renewed efforts to create a nationwide registry system, which was now logistically possible because of the considerable progress the government had made in suppressing rebels in the provinces. Such a nationwide registry was a necessary precondition for conscription.

On 17 Ḥut [Esfand] 1303 / 8 March 1925, the parliament held the first

47. Gholām-Ḥoseyn Mirzā Ṣāleḥ, ed., *Reżā Shāh: Khāṭerāt-e Soleymān-e Behbudi, Shams-e Pahlavi, 'Ali-ye Izadi* (Tehran: Tarḥ-e Now, 1372/1993), 121–122. The date of the entry is 27 Ḥut [Esfand] 1302 / 18 March 1924. The sender of this letter was a popular preacher by the name of Āqā Jamāl, who was one of the ringleaders of the anti-republican movement on the streets.

48. Sālur, *Ruznāmeh*, volume 9 (1379/2000), 7256 and 7270.

49. Reżā Niyāzmand, *Reżā Shāh az tavallod tā salṭanat* (Tehran: Enteshārāt-e Jāme'eh-ye Irāniyān, 1381/2002), 658–661.

50. See Vanessa Martin, "Mudarris, Republicanism and the Rise to Power of Riza Khan, Sardar Sipah," *Bulletin of the British Society for Middle Eastern Studies* 21:2 (1994): 200–211.

reading of a new law on *sejell-e aḥvāl.*[51] After much debate about the name of the institution, which was deemed unfamiliar to most people, the first article was approved. Article 2 stated that all those who had been born before the law had to get an identity document (*sejell*, colloquially called *sejeld*) and that, if they were minors, the head of the family had to obtain one for them. Noṣrat al-Dowleh pointed out the ambiguity of the term *khānevādeh* (family), which included so many people that it was not clear who the head might be (the word obviously had the connotation of what we would today call "extended family"), and suggested replacing the term with *'ā'eleh* (household), which consisted of a man, his wife, children, manservants (*nowkar*), and maidservants (*kolfat*).[52] On the next day the third article was approved; it said that for an illiterate person, the registry official had to fill out the form in the presence of two trusted persons. The rapporteur, Mirzā Shehāb al-Din, explained that the presence of the two was required because if it was only one, that one might go and claim to be someone's son, get papers, and then claim inheritance after that person's death. Then Article 4, which is of direct interest to this study, was voted on. The proposal read: "Every head of family (*khānevādeh*) has to choose a name for his family by which all family members will be known. Thus every person will have a name consisting of a family name and a personal name, for instance Eskandar Ebrāhim, where Eskandar is the personal name and Ebrāhim is the family name." The deputy Āqā Seyyed Ya'qub acknowledged that it was important to register people's names, because the state needed to know who was who and how many people there were, but wondered why it was necessary to force people to add a name to the name their parents had given them. The rapporteur explained that in Tehran there might be ten thousand Ḥoseyns, and they had to be distinguished somehow.[53] And to keep lineages and families protected, the second name should be borne by the entire family. One deputy, Yāsā'i, suggested prohibiting the adoption of the names of famous figures from the past like Sa'di and Ferdowsi, but 'Ali Akbar Dāvar said that people should be free to choose whatever name they liked. The issue of the definition of *khānevādeh* was raised again, but was not resolved, as the whole article was sent back to the committee. Article 5 came up for discussion next. It read: "Titles will always be registered in the identity document after the name, and the registry official has to examine the granting document" (*sanad-e*

51. *Moẕākerāt-e Majles-e Showrā-ye Melli, dowreh-ye panjom* (Tehran: Edāreh-ye ruznāmeh-ye rasmi-ye keshvar-e shāhanshāhi-ye Irān, n.d.), 964.

52. Ibid, 966.

53. Cf. the Siamese king's rhetorical question: if one commune had ten people named Di, how could the good Di be told from the bad one? Walter F. Vella, *Chaiyo!: King Vajiravudh and the Development of Thai Nationalism* (Honolulu: The University Press of Hawaii, 1978), 130.

laqab), which conformed to the 1918 law. This article was easily passed. Then more articles, concerning the technicalities of registering life events, were approved, aspects of the law that, while very important, have no bearing on the present study.

Parliamentary debate on the law resumed on 11 Farvardin / 31 March 1925, the same day on which a law was passed instituting Persian names for the twelve solar months (Farvardin etc.) in lieu of the old signs of the zodiac. Article 4 of the *sejell-e aḥvāl* law, which had been sent back to the commission, was now approved in slightly altered form. The words "every family head" were replaced with the words "every person" (meaning, in fact, every *man*), and so "family head" came to be defined as a man who had children and grandchildren. The article now read:

> Every person must choose a special name for himself. His wife and all male children and grandchildren, as well as all female children and grandchildren so long as they have not married, will be named by that special name, which is their family name. Thus every person will have a name consisting of a family name and a personal name, for instance "Iraj Kāvus," where Iraj is the personal name and Kāvus the family name. Persons who are of a single lineage (*nasl-e vāḥed*) can choose the same name for themselves, and children and grandchildren of such a family head who are not under his guardianship can choose separate names for themselves. Note: After registration in the Registry Office, the family name is reserved for people who have registered it, and other people may not adopt it in that location.[54]

It is clear from this wording that during the time that Article 4 had been debated in the commission, the name of the generic Iranian had changed from Eskandar Ebrāhim to Iraj Kāvus, a Persianization that was probably not unrelated to the adoption of the Persian names for the twelve months of the solar calendar.

But before the law could be finalized, another law was passed rendering Article 5 of the law obsolete. On 11 Ordibehesht 1304 / 1 May 1925, the newspaper *Irān* reported that Reżā Pahlavi, the prime minister and commander-in-chief,[55] had given orders that all titles be abolished in the military, and that a circular had been sent to all state offices ordering discontinuation of

54. *Majmu'eh-ye qavānin-e mowżu'eh va moṣavvabāt-e dowreh-ye panjom-e taqniniyeh* (Tehran: Maṭba'eh-ye Majles, n.d.), 37.

55. The constitution granted this title to the shah, but as part of the creeping ouster of the Qājārs, the parliamentary majority had voted to name the prime minister commander-in-chief on 25 Bahman 1303 / 14 February 1925. Shaji'i, *Nokhbegān-e siyāsi-ye Irān*, volume 3, 153.

their use. As to his person, he should be mentioned by his rank in all official correspondence and by his family name, Pahlavi, in all private correspondence.[56] At this point, some title holders realized what was coming and began putting notices in the newspapers asking people to stop addressing them by their titles as well. The abovementioned Showkat al-Solṭān now disowned his title completely: "I ask my friends to forget my title, Showkat al-Solṭān, and to call me by my original name, Seyyed Asad Allāh Khān Mojarrad." Next to that we find a notice by the governor of Savojbolāgh: "I ask those gentlemen who know me henceforth to address me by my family name, Mirzā 'Ali Khān Farhādi." But it is signed "Amjad al-Solṭān" (Most Lauded of the Ruler) (Figure 11).[57]

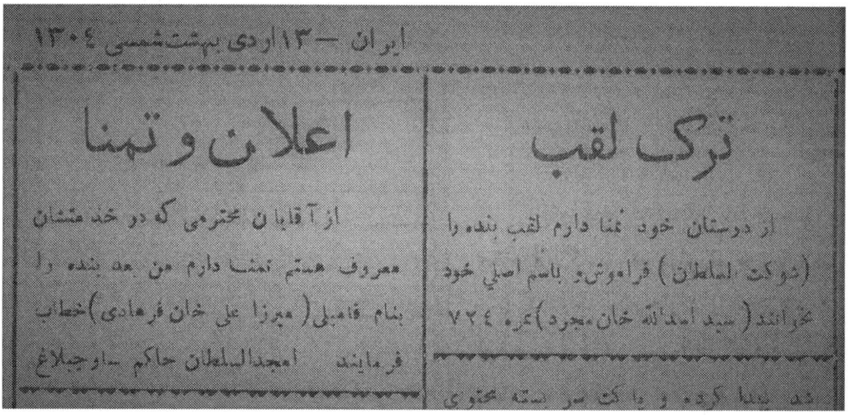

ایران — ۱۳ اردی بهشت شمسی ۱۳۰۴

ترک لقب

از دوستان خود تمنا دارم لقب بنده را
(شوکت السلطان) فراموش و باسم اصلی خود
بخوانند (سید اسدالله خان مجرد) عره ۷۲۴

اعلان و تمنا

از آقایان محترمی که در خدمتشان
معروف هستم تمنا دارم من بعد بنده را
بنام فامیلی (میرزا علی خان فرهادی) خطاب
فرمایند امجدالسلطان حاکم ساوجبلاغ

Figure 11: Confusion?

To give legal effect to the order to discontinue the use of titles, on 15 Ordibehesht 1304 / 5 May 1925 the cabinet introduced a bill in parliament proposing that all titles and ranks (*manāseb*) containing the words "*Sepahsālār*, *Sepahdār*, *Sardār*, *Sepahbod*, *Amir Tumān*, *Amir Yunān*, *Amir Panj*, as well as all other titles that contain the words *Sepāh*, *Lashkar*, *Jang*, *Sālār*, or *Neẓām* be abolished."[58] This measure was justified by the creation of a modern army and by the fact that many military-sounding titles had been given to people who had nothing to do with the army, which devalued titles that ought to represent a reward for sacrifice and valor. A majority of the

56. "Elghā'e alqāb," *Irān*, 11 Ordibehesht 1304 / 1 May 1925, 2.
57. *Irān*, 13 Ordibehesht / 3 May 1925, 3.
58. The following account of this day's debates is from *Mozākerat-e Majles Showrā-ye Melli, dowreh-ye panjom*, 1105–1110.

deputies requested urgency (*fowriat*) for this measure, and so the debate began. Taqizādeh opened the substantive debate. He expressed approval for the bill, saying, en passant, that *all* titles should be abolished but calling for the preservation of *Sepahsālār*, *Sepahbod*, *Sardār*, and *Sālār*, as these were old Iranian titles attested since Achaemenean and Sasanian times that could be used to designate officer ranks in the military. The minister of finance, Forughi, intervened to say that the government only wanted to abolish their use as purely honorific titles, and that the designation of ranks in the military should be left to the government and the ministry of war. Taqizādeh's suggestion to keep the four titles was voted down. Then the deputy Shirvāni suggested that *Farmānfarmā* (Giver of Orders) be added to the list, eliciting a sharp reply from Sālār Lashkar (Leader of the Army), the second son of Prince 'Abd al-Ḥoseyn Farmānfarmā and brother of Noṣrat al-Dowleh, who called this proposal a personal attack on his family which had nothing to do with state affairs or the progress of the army. Shirvāni responded that he was forced to doubt His Highness's allegation, as he probably had a closer acquaintance with the current holder of the title than His Highness, eliciting chuckles from the deputies.[59] The title of *Farmānfarmā* was mentioned in the constitution,[60] he said, but Sālār Lashkar was free to choose it as his family name, if he so desired.[61] Shirvāni's proposal was voted down too. Then Shirvāni suggested that a second article be added to the bill, outlawing the future bestowal of any of the titles mentioned in Article 1. The proposal was voted down, but when Dāvar made a similar suggestion, it was approved.

Discussion then turned to titles in general. Sarkashikzādeh suggested that the bestowal of new titles of all sorts (both military and civilian) be stopped, so that they might die out in fifty years. But two deputies, Reżā Dāmghāni and Modir al-Molk (Manager of the Realm, who would be prime minister as Maḥmud Jam from 1935 to 1939), suggested abolishing all titles immediately. [Prince] 'Emād al-Salṭaneh (Pillar of the Monarchy), who does not seem to have shared his bother 'Eyn al-Salṭaneh's jaundiced view of titles, objected that the general abolition of titles was unconstitutional and pointed out that in the future it might be necessary for the government to bestow them. Besides, the government would have included such a

59. Sālār Lashkar was somewhat estranged from his father at that time. Private communication from the historian Mansoureh Ettehadieh (Nezam-Mafi), Sālār Lashkar's granddaughter, 17 March 2007.

60. His reasoning is opaque, but he probably meant that the governors of major provinces (*ayālats*) are called *farmānfarmā*, for which reason the word should not be used as a title.

61. Sālār Lashkar did in fact take Farmānfarmā as his family name, unlike his older brother, Noṣrat al-Dowleh, who chose the name Firuz.

measure (abolishing titles) in its original bill had it found it necessary to do so, wherefore the deputies should content themselves with what the cabinet had proposed. Sarkashizādeh's proposal was voted down.

Then Dāmghāni took the floor again. He stated that names are not specific to those who bear them, but titles are. The prophet Moses was called Kalim Allāh because God spoke to him. Titles must have a raison d'être, but in a country that has become decadent and weak they are empty phrases. At the end of the 'Abbāsid era, he averred, when Iran was divided into small statelets (*moluk al-tavā'ef*) and disorder reigned, titles had appeared that persisted to the present (a reference to the Buyids). This trend had become more pronounced in the recent period of despotism (*estebdād*), and since the whole world was making fun of the meaningless titles of Iran, they should be abolished. Besides, people were now assuming titles themselves, besmirching the identities of those who had earned them. If someone has earned merit, his scientific works and record should be the indicators of that merit, not titles. Now that military titles are abolished, why discriminate in favor of civilian ones? Dāmghāni's proposal was voted down, after which the meeting was adjourned for a pause.

When the chamber reconvened, Zeyn al-'Ābedin Rahnamā took the floor. He reported that outside the chamber during the break, most deputies had agreed that titles were useless. In fact, while the deputies were outside, Rahnamā, Dāvar, Taqizādeh, 'Alā'i, and Shari'atzādeh had agreed on a new formula,[62] which Rahnamā presented to the Speaker. He said that if titles were given for merit, there would not be so many of them, and that the sheer quantity of them was something that the press, newspapers, and books in Europe made fun of. To illustrate his point, he reported that he had recently been sent a book from Paris titled *Shāh-e Mogholestān* (The King of Mongolia), which provided literal translations of fantasy titles and poked fun at Iranians.[63] Moḥammad Vali Mirzā, the third son of Prince Farmānfarmā, responded that the deputies were wasting their time and should leave those who had titles alone. He surmised that those who were proposing the abolition of titles just wanted to be known as *tip-e motejadded* (modernist types, but perhaps also a reference to the Tajaddod party). The people's pulse, he averred, had not stopped beating (*nabż-e mellat sāqeṭ nashodeh*) and the nation was not holding its breath waiting to see what the majles would do. He

62. The identities of the deputies who spearheaded the move are not given in the parliamentary debates, but they are listed in the official newspaper's report on the session: "Yek jalaseh-ye por-ḥarārat," *Irān*, 16 Ordibehesht 1304 / 6 May 1925, 2.

63. This is of course *Le Chah du Mahboulistan*, mentioned above.

further suggested that the promoters of abolition were in league with the press, craving the income from the notices in which people would announce their new names. This enraged a number of deputies, who called this an attack on culture, and Dāvar got up and said that Moḥammad Vali Mirzā was right in pointing out that the nation's pulse had not stopped beating and that it was therefore not expecting parliament to act upon the issue. But the reason for this lack of expectation was that people like the prince had for years kept the people in a mental state where they did not realize what needed to be done and what did not. A vote was called, and a third article, which read "All civilian (*keshvari*) titles are abolished three months after the passing of this article," was approved. The final speaker was the deputy for Yazd, Abolḥasan Hā'erizādeh, a cleric and member of the minority faction. He pointed out that no one in his family bore a title but said that he thought this was an unwarranted interference in people's lives, and if there were too many titles, the cabinet should request that the Court bestow fewer of them. At long last, the minister of finance, Moḥammad 'Ali Forughi, got up and said that the government agreed with parliament's decision, as titles were neither indicators of service nor of merit, and those who bore them hated them. He called for a vote on the entire law, which passed when a majority of deputies stood up.

The next day, *Irān*, ever enthusiastic about modernizing change, likened the "historic vote" to that taken in the French Constituent Assembly on 4 August 1789 (when the Declaration of the Rights of Man and the Citizen was issued and the privileges of the nobility and the clergy were abolished), ascribing the outcome to a coalition of leftist and freedom-loving forces united against reaction.[64] The issue announcing the law included seven public notices indicating the names by which former title holders now wanted to be known. Such notices continued in subsequent issues, until on 27 Ordibehesht 1304 / 17 May 1925 the newspaper, "to comply with the wishes of a number of subscribers," started publishing tables of correspondences between titles and names in which the country's most important statesmen were listed.[65] While some of the new names consisted of a forename and a surname, as stipulated in the *sejell-e aḥvāl* law (which had not yet taken effect), some high-born notables included the honorific *Khān* as part of their name. Some seemed to wish to distinguish between the surname by which they wanted to be known and the official family name they had registered at the *sejell-e aḥvāl*: "From this date my name and signature (*emżā'*) will be 'Abd al-'Ali Rażavi, and my family name Mirzā'i. [Signed:] Neẓām al-Towliyeh"

64. "Yek jalaseh-ye por-ḥarārat," *Irān*, 16 Ordibehesht 1304 / 6 May 1925, 1–2.
65. *Irān*, 27 Ordibehesht 1304 / 17 May 1925, 1.

(Order of the Administration) (Figure 12).[66] By the late summer of 1925, individual announcements began petering out.

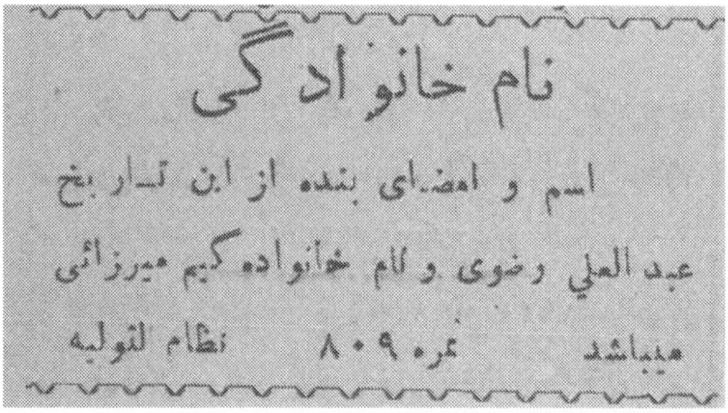

نام خانوادگی

اسم و امضای بنده از این تاریخ

عبد العلی رضوی و نام خانواده کریم میرزائی

میباشد نمره ۸۰۹ نظام التولیه

Figure 12: Distinction between signature and surname

That the abolition of the titles was part and parcel of the ongoing campaign to prepare public opinion for the toppling of the Qājār dynasty can be gleaned from an article in *Ḥabl al-Matin* that celebrated the simplification of official language and ended with the ominous question: "what benefit have we derived for the last hundred and fifty years from the use of a useless word like *Qebleh-ye ʻĀlam*?" The "hundred and fifty years" corresponded to the Qājār dynasty, and *Qebleh-ye ʻĀlam* (kibla [= focus point] of the world) was one of the titles of the shah.[67]

The *sejell-e aḥvāl* law became the law of the land on 14 Khordād 1304 / 4 June 1925, when the final two articles were voted on.[68] Only two days later the new conscription law was passed: the state had to know the age and place of residence of young men before they could be drafted. Article 6 of this law said: "At the beginning of each [Solar Hijri] year, until the end of Farvardin [20 April], the conscription office of each military region shall extract a list of individuals [= men] who reach conscription age that year ... from that region's registry office and ... send it to the ministry of war."[69] The law contained provisions for exemption from military service based on family relationships, which also made the registration of those relationships necessary.

66. *Irān*, 20 Ordibehesht 1304 / 10 May 1925, 1. Neẓām al-Towliyeh was perhaps more inclined to go by his *nisba*, which linked him to the eighth Imam, than by his family name.

67. *Ḥabl al-Matin*, 17 August 1925, as quoted in "A propos de la suppression officielle des titres honorifiques," *Revue du monde musulman* 61 (1925): 172.

68. Moẕākerat-e Majles Showrā-ye Melli, dowreh-ye panjom, 1252–1253.

69. *Majmuʻeh-ye qavānin-e mowżuʻeh va moṣavvabāt-e dowreh-ye panjom-e taqniniyeh* (Tehran: Matbaʻeh-ye Majles, n.d.), 42. The original reads: *shoʻbeh-ye sarbāzgiri-ye har nāḥiyeh-ye qoshuni ṣurati az kolliyeh-ye afrādi keh dar ān sāl beh senn-e sarbāzi miresand va dar s̱abt-e ḥowżeh-hā-ye joz' mibāshand az daftar-e sejell-e ān nāḥiyeh estekhrāj namudeh va be vasileh-ye ro'asā-ye māfowq-e khod be vezārat-e jang ersāl midārad.*

Much has been written about Iran's experience with conscription after 1925;[70] I mention it here only to emphasize the fact that in Iran, as elsewhere, there was a close connection between military concerns and the laws that standardized naming practices. There can be little doubt that preparing the ground for an efficient system of conscription was a more important motivation for the *sejell-e aḥvāl* law than making sure that every Iranian had a family name, as the adoption of family names had been gaining ground anyway. By late summer 1925, thirteen thousand surnames had been registered in Tehran.[71]

Without acknowledging this link it would be impossible to account for the adoption of a third *sejell-e aḥvāl* law in the summer of 1928 (20 Mordād 1928).[72] The shortcomings of the 1925 law can be gleaned from the parliamentary debate which preceded the adoption of the law in 1928. According to a number of deputies, the inadequate implementation of the law had led to much hardship in the population. For instance, many people did not know their age, and the local registry officials then simply assigned them one. But this led to old men and young boys being drafted. Many registry officials had also enriched themselves by taking bribes.[73] The new law, which superseded the one passed in 1925, was passed by the Sixth Majles on 20 Mordād 1307 / 11 August 1928.[74] Its first article stated that women had to obtain identity papers in person or through their attorneys. But none of these shortcomings, nor the remedies found for them, concerned the provisions on names, and the only changes between the laws of 1925 and 1928 regarding naming practices were that the article about titles was dropped, titles having been abolished in the meantime, and that the name of the generic Iranian man was once again changed (this time to Maḥmud Kāmrān, a combination containing an Arab forename and a Persian surname). The bylaws for this law were adopted by the cabinet on 27 Khordād 1307 / 17 June 1928. Article 45 allowed a person who wanted to change his or her surname to make such a request in written form to the local registry; the local registry would then convey the request to the central registry in Tehran, which would decide on the admissibility of the request.[75]

70. Stephanie Cronin, "Conscription and Popular Resistance in Iran, 1925–1941," *International Review of Social History* 43:3 (1998): 451–471.

71. Sālur, *Ruznāmeh*, volume 9 (1379/2000), 7312.

72. *Majmu'eh-ye qavānin-e mowżu'eh va masā'el-e moṣavvabeh-ye dowreh-ye sheshom-e taqniniyeh* (Tehran: Maṭba'eh-ye Majles, n.d.), 257–264.

73. *Mozākerāt-e Majles, Dowreh-e sheshom-e taqniniyeh, jalaseh-ye 220* (Tehran: Maṭba'eh-ye Majles, n.d.), 3873–3885.

74. For the text of the law, see 'Abbās Mirshekāri, *Tabār-shenāsi-ye ḥoqūq-e sabt-e aḥvāl: moshtamal bar: qavānin, moqarrarāt va ārā-ye vaḥdat-e raviyeh dar ḥowzeh-ye ḥoqūq-e sabt-e aḥvāl az āghāz tā konun* (Tehran: Enteshārāt-e Jāvdāneh, 1393/2014), 15–20.

75. "Neẓām-nāmeh-ye sejell-e aḥvāl," reprinted in Mirshekāri, *Tabār-shenāsi*, 57.

Apparently even this new legislation did not achieve the desired results as to the behavior of registry officials, for in March 1931 / Esfand 1309, the parliament passed a law placing registry officials who had committed acts of embezzlement or allowed themselves to be bribed in the hands of military courts, on a par with delinquent police officials.[76]

The 1935 Circular on Honorifics

It may or may not be a coincidence that a decree outlawing the last vestiges of traditional titulature in Iran was issued a year after Reżā Shah's return from Turkey. This trip, Reżā Shah's only state visit abroad, was the culmination of a gradual improvement in Turkish-Iranian relations and afforded the shah an opportunity to witness the extent to which the Europeanization of public life had progressed in Turkey.[77] As a result, to allow Iran to catch up, the pace of cultural reforms was accelerated in Iran after his return, most visibly in the forced adoption of the brimmed hat for men and the abolition of veiling for women.[78]

On 9 Mordād 1314 / 1 August 1935, the ministry of justice announced a new set of reforms in a circular that standardized a number of honorifics (*'anāvin*) while abolishing others. To justify the measure, it was stated that the use of these long-winded *'anāvin* was a relic of former times and did not correspond to the requirements of the times, and that the time spent on phrase-mongering should instead be spent on useful pursuits. The only admissible honorifics were to be *Āqā* (= Mister) and *Khānom* (= Mrs. or Miss).[79]

Article 1 fixed the styles of office of the ruling family: *a'lāḥażrat-e homāyuni-ye shāhanshāhi* for the Shah, *olyāḥażrat* for the Queen, *vālāḥażrat-e homāyuni* for the Crown Prince, and *vālāḥażrat* for the *shāhpurs* and *shāhdokhts*, i.e., sons and daughters of the shah. These honorifics were a continuation but also a modification of Qajar practice. *A'lāḥażrat* had been used for the Qajar monarchs, but since there were no official queens under that dynasty, its feminine equivalent, *'olyāḥażrat,* must have been either coined for Reżā Shah's consort or imported from India, where it had been used for Queen Victoria.[80] *Vālāḥażrat* inverted the Qajar *ḥażrat-e vālā*,

76. "Qānun-e marja'-e moḥākemeh-ye ma'murin-e nażmiyeh va sejell-e aḥvāl," reprinted in ibid., 20.

77. Afshin Marashi, "Performing the Nation: The Shah's Official State Visit to Kemalist Turkey, June to July 1934," in Stephanie Cronin, ed., *The Making of Modern Iran* (London: Routledge, 2003), 99–119.

78. Houchang E. Chehabi, "Staging the Emperor's New Clothes," *Iranian Studies* 26:3–4 (Summer/Fall 1993): 209–233.

79. *Mottaḥed al-ma'āl*, dated 9 Mordād 1314 (1 August 1935), in *Majalleh-ye rasmi-ye vezārat-e 'adliyeh*, no. 1964, 14 Mordād 1314, 1 and 2.

80. Personal observation, Victoria Memorial, Calcutta, 26 December 2015.

while *shāhpur* and *shāhdokht* replaced the Qajar *shāhzādeh* (colloquially pronounced *shāzdeh*). *Homāyun*, meaning "imperial" in this context, signaled the imperial (rather than royal) rank of the Shāhanshāh, "King of the Kings," a title that was considered in Europe to be the equivalent of "Emperor" (like the Ethiopian *Negus Negesti*). As for high officials of the Iranian state, the names of the prime minister, the speaker of parliament, cabinet members, and ambassadors were preceded by the term *jenāb*, and when they were addressed directly, *jenāb(-e) 'āli* was to replace the personal pronoun. For other state officials the appropriate style became the common *Āqā* for men and *Khānom* for women, and in direct speech they were to be addressed with the polite second-person personal pronoun *shomā*, "you."

Article 2 abolished the honorifics attached to cities, ministries, and state administrations. Examples given were *Dār al-Khelāfeh* (Abode of the Caliphate) for Tehran,[81] *Vezārat-e jalileh-ye dākheleh* (Illustrious Ministry of the Interior), *Edāreh-ye moḥtarameh-ye ṣeḥḥiyeh* (Honorable Public Health Office), and *Postkhāneh-ye mobārakeh* (Auspicious Post Office).

Article 3 abolished honorifics that preceded names, such as *ḥożur-e mobārak* (auspicious presence), *maqām-e mani'* (impregnable rank), or *sāḥat-e moḥtaram* (honorable grounds), and invocatory phrases that were placed after names, such as *shayyada Allāhu arkānahu* (may God strengthen his pillars [of power]) and *dāmat 'aẓamatuh* (may his grandeur last).[82]

Article 4 had a direct bearing on onomastics *stricto sensu*, as it abolished the titles *Mirzā*, *Khān*, *Beyk*, and *Amir* (the equivalents of titles outlawed in Turkey a year earlier) either before or after a name.

Article 5, finally, fixed the styles of address for foreign dignitaries, establishing a certain homology between international usage and Iranian teminology. Emperors were to be styled *a'lāḥażrat-e emperāṭuri* (Imperial Majesty), kings *a'lāḥażrat* (Majesty). Regents, reigning princes, the Nizam of Hyderabad, and other Indian maharajas were to be addressed as *vālāḥażrat*, a word which became the equivalent of "Highness" since it was also used for

81. The title *Dār al-Khelāfeh*, not uncommon in the later Islamic period in Sunni lands, had been given to Tehran perhaps to spite the Ottomans, whose rulers were also caliphs. Other cities bore titles such as *Dār al-Marz* (Abode of the Border: Rasht) and *Dār al-Salṭaneh* (Abode of the Monarchy: Tabriz). For the history of these titles see Ashraf, "Laqab va 'onvān": 299–303. Today such titles can still be found in Malaysia, where a number of peninsular states carry them, e.g. Johor Darul Ta'zim.

82. The irony was that on the same page of the official gazette of the ministry of justice, another circular, abolishing the use of the term *mamlekati* ("pertaining to the state"), refers to the royal order inspiring this measure as "*amr-e moṭā'-e molukāneh, arvāḥonā fadāh*," "the to-be-obeyed order of the shah, may our souls be sacrificed to him." *Mottaḥed al-ma'āl*, dated 9 Mordād 1314 (1 August 1935), in *Majalleh-ye rasmi-ye vezārat-e 'adliyeh*, no. 1964, 14 Mordād 1314, 1.

the offspring of the Shah. Presidents were to be styled *ḥażrat*, as were prime ministers, speakers of parliament, government ministers, ambassadors, and ministers plenipotentiary (a diplomatic rank, which has since been abolished, for heads of mission below the rank of ambassador). This became the equivalent of "Excellency."

A few days after the publication of this decree, the daily newspaper *Eṭṭelā'āt*, which had by now replaced *Irān* as the mouthpiece of state-sponsored modernism,[83] celebrated this measure in an article that imputed the use of the outlawed terms, formulas, and phrases to the idleness and sycophancy that characterized the past but were no longer compatible with the spirit of the age, which called for work and activity: "*The program of the government is work*, and the people must make work the program of their lives."[84]

Later Modifications

Shortly after this last measure, a new installment of Iran's Civil Code, namely Book 3 of Volume 2, was promulgated by parliament.[85] It contained ten articles about identity papers (Articles 992–1001). Article 993 specified the following life events that had to be registered with the civil registry: 1. births and abortions; 2. marriages, both permanent and temporary; 3. divorces, both permanent and revocable; and 4. death. Article 997 said that everybody had to have a family name, and Article 998 allowed people whose surname had been adopted by someone else without permission to sue and oblige the other person to change his name.[86]

The laws and circulars discussed so far essentially established the onomastic regime that is still in place today. Since then, a number of laws, bylaws, amendments, circulars, and ordinances have only slightly modified the basic rules regarding family names and honorifics.

On 4 September 1935 / 12 Shahrivar 1314 the cabinet issued new bylaws for the Registry Office. Its Chapter 7 included eight articles specifying the bureaucratic procedures for changing forenames and surnames. By now, people were also inheriting surnames rather than adopting them, and the

83. See Bianca Devos, *Presse und Unternehmertum in Iran: die Tageszeitung Ittilā'āt in der frühen Pahlavī-Zeit* (Würzburg: Ergon Verlag, 2012).

84. "Elghā-ye 'anāvin va alqāb," *Eṭṭelā'āt*, 11 Mordād 1314/2 August 1935. Emphasis in the original.

85. For a brief account of the elaboration of a Civil Code in the wake of the Constitutional Revolution see Ali Gheissari, "Constitutional Rights and the Development of Civil Law in Iran," in H. E. Chehabi and Vanessa Martin, eds., *Iran's Constitutional Revolution: Politics, Cultural Transformations and Transnational Connections* (London: I.B. Tauris, 2010), 74–76.

86. *Qānun-e madani* (Tehran: Mo'asseseh-ye maṭbu'āti-ye Amir Kabir, 1333/1954), 129–130; Mirshekāri, *Tabār-shenāsi*, 22–24.

new bylaws established that the heirs of a deceased man inherited his exclusive right to the registered family name in their locality, although they were free jointly to grant permission to someone else in that locality to adopt it.[87] With those procedures in place, a few months later, on 12 April 1937 / 23 Farvardin 1316, a new set of bylaws was issued; Article 108 restricted the choice of family names by specifying the types of surnames that could not be adopted and obliging all those who were already carrying such names to change them. Forbidden were surnames related to the imperial family or to the titles and honorifics of high state officials; registered names of companies and commercial enterprises; ugly, unpleasant, or obscene names; surnames that looked like titles; words related to foreign languages; and finally, surnames that were composed of a family name that was already registered and a small addition.[88]

And families complied with the restrictions. Decades later, Holāku Rāmbod, the leader of the parliamentary caucus of the "opposition" Mardom Party under Moḥammad Reżā Shah, recalled that when he was doing his military service, an order came that words like *Amir*, *Khān*, and *Mirzā* had to be deleted from family names; their family surname was Khāntālesh, and he changed his to Rāmbod, while his older brother chose Bābākhānlu.[89] The prohibition on foreign words led various members of the Kāshānski family, likewise, to adopt the surnames Sudāvar, Kāshāni, and Key-Āshiyān.[90]

A few months after the publication of these bylaws, the semiofficial newspaper *Eṭṭelā'āt* printed an article titled "Family Name" to justify the purging of foreign words, complaining that too many surnames were not purely Persian and insisting that an Iranian's name should reflect the heritage of his glorious civilization.[91]

A number of further laws that had a bearing on names were later adopted in Iran. On 22 Ordibehesht 1319 / 12 May 1940, parliament passed a law to reform the registry system that again contained a chapter on family names. Article 41 stated that children born in a place other than the one where their father had registered the surname were entitled to their father's family name, even if there was a different family bearing that name in their place of birth. Article 42 made it much more difficult to change one's

87. "Neẓām-nāmeh-ye edāreh-ye koll-e eḥṣā'iyeh va sejell-e aḥvāl," Mirshekāri, *Tabār-shenāsi*, 84–85.

88. "Neẓām-nāmeh-ye qānun-e s̱abt-e aḥvāl," Mirshekāri, *Tabār-shenāsi*, 106–107.

89. Moṣṭafā Alamuti, *Irān dar 'aṣr-e Pahlavi*, volume 12 (London: Book Press, 1992), 218.

90. Fatema Soudavar, personal e-mail communication, 11 March 2015, and Abolala Soudavar, personal e-mail communication, 25 July 2015.

91. "Nām-e khānevādegi," *Eṭṭelā'āt*, 24 Āẕar 1316 / 15 December 1937.

surname: only the shah himself could grant permission for it.[92] To adopt a different surname, one had to make a request to the Ministry of the Interior giving the reasons; if approved, the request would then be submitted by the prime minister to the shah. Finally, article 43 allowed a divorced woman to retain her ex-husband's surname only with his permission, adding that likewise, if a man had adopted his wife's surname, she had to consent to him keeping it after a divorce.[93]

In 1976 the registry system was thoroughly overhauled with a new law, which survived the Islamic Revolution of 1979 and remains in force to this day, albeit in amended form. The 1976 law had nothing new to say about names, but the amendments approved by the Islamic Consultative Assembly of the Islamic Republic in January 1985 did. Article 20 of the law had given the right to give a newborn a first name to whoever registered the birth. Six amendments were added to this article. Parents' choice was henceforth restricted, as forenames that insulted Islam, were obscene, or did not accord with the sex of the child were prohibited. Three amendments concerned the "recognized religious minorities" (Zoroastrians, Jews, and Christians), which was in line with the Islamic Republic's general policy of treating Muslims and non-Muslims differentially. It was their own "language and religious culture" that were to determine the appropriateness of their given names; their religion had to be noted in their identity papers and if they converted to Islam, the date of their conversion and their new first and last names had to be entered into their identity papers as well. Finally, it became obligatory to register a person's status as a *seyyed* (descendant of the Prophet) in their identity document if their father's or grandfather's identity documents contained that status. Exceptions were made for people who did not consider themselves *seyyed*s or whose *seyyed*hood had been disproven according to sharia rules.[94] While there was a lengthy discussion in parliament about restricting parents' right to name their children, no one spoke against the amendments concerning non-Muslims and *seyyeds*.[95]

Since 1985, a number of ordinances (*dastur al-'amal*) have elaborated on the criteria that render a first name "insulting to Islam" or "obscene." Interestingly, a 1985 ordinance allowed men whose forename was composed

92. One might speculate about whether this rather odd provision might have been occasioned by the onomastic complications arising from the marriages of Reżā Shah's daughters, to be discussed below.

93. "Qānun-e eṣlāḥ-e qānun-e s̱abt-e aḥvāl," Mirshekāri, *Tabār-shenāsi*, 32–33.

94. "Qānun-e s̱abt-e aḥvāl," Mirshekāri, *Tabār-shenāsi*, 132–133.

95. *Mashruḥ-e moẕākerāt-e majles-e showrā-ye eslāmi, dowreh-ye dovvom, 1161* (Tehran: n.p., 1363/1984), 24–33.

of the word *'abd* (slave) plus another given name, e.g., 'Abd al-'Ali, to drop the first part, since that "suffix is reserved for the names and qualities of the Creator."[96] This may have been in response to occasional Sunni criticisms that Shiites elevated their Imams to quasi-divine status. In 2009 another ordinance regarding given names outlawed the dropping of the word *'abd* when connected to a divine name or attribute, such as 'Abd al-Raḥim.[97] Finally, in 2012, yet another ordinance added to the list of prohibited names.[98] The quickening pace of these regulations may reflect the social changes in Iranian society, where some people changed their Persian names to Muslim names in response to the state's Islamization drive while others were precisely rebelling against this policy by dropping religious elements from their names.

96. "Dastur al-'amal-e marbuṭ beh taghyir-e nām," Mirshekāri, *Tabār-shenāsi*, 166.
97. "Dastur al-'amal-e nām," Mirshekāri, *Tabār-shenāsi*, 219.
98. "Dastur al-'amal-e taghyir-e nām," Mirshekāri, *Tabār-shenāsi*, 221–224.

4

POST-1925 NAMING PRACTICES

The actual implementation of the reform measures did not always follow the path intended by the reformers. We will first look at the actual names Iranians took, then examine the social consequences of the new onomastic regime, and end with a few comparative remarks that put the Iranian experience in a wider context.

Iranian Surnames

Let us begin with the surname of the man who is most identified with state-led modernization in twentieth-century Iran, Reżā Shah. Much has been said and implied about why he chose the surname Pahlavi, most notably that it was his well-known love for pre-Islamic Iranian history that determined the choice, Pahlavi (one of the dialects of Middle Persian) having been the official language of the Sasanian empire. This fact probably helped, but does not in and of itself explain the choice, for one does not usually name oneself after a language. In fact, there was more to the choice.

To begin with, the Mazandaran village in which Reżā Khān was born, Ālāsht, had a number of quarters, and the one in which his family resided bore the name of Pahlavān Kheyl.[1] *Pahlavān*, a noun related to *Pahlavi*, means "hero" in Persian, an association that cannot have been unwelcome. The clan to which Reżā Khān's paternal family belonged was called Pālāni, and it seems that a number of historians told Reżā Khān that when the Arabs attacked Iran, some Sasanians retreated to the Alborz mountains, where they settled in Ālāsht, and that the name of these Sasanians was Pahlavi, which over time became Pālāni in the local dialect. Furthermore, they pointed out, there was a cave not far from Ālāsht which contained inscriptions in Pahlavi. Reżā Khān reportedly liked this line of reasoning and therefore chose the name Pahlavi for himself.[2] Another story is told by the German diplomat Wipert von Blücher, who wrote in his memoirs that Reżā Khān once asked

1. Doktor Reżā Niyāzmand, *Reżā Shāh az tavallod tā salṭanat* (Tehran: Enteshārāt-e Jāme'eh-ye Irāniyān, 1381/2002), 15.
2. Ibid., 44.

the German Orientalist and archaeologist Ernst Herzfeld while they were together in a tent what the word "Pahlavi" meant, to which Herzfeld responded that it denoted both a medieval language and an inhabitant of Khorasan, and could have the sense of "heroic."[3]

Once Reżā Shah had ascended the throne, he insisted that no one else be called Pahlavi. When his relatives wanted to adopt his surname after 1925, he ordered them to take Pahlawnezhād instead. Matters did not rest there, however. In 1941 two of Reżā Shah's daughters remarried and requested to adopt the name Pahlavinezhād, which the new Shah granted. But in order for them not to be confused with their paternal cousins, the latter were asked to change their name again, this time from Pahlawnezhād to Pahlavān. In the meantime, however, some other people in Mazandaran had chosen the family name Pahlavān; they in turn were also told to take a different surname.[4]

As for the members of the old dynasty, only a few took Qājār as a surname, notably the immediate relatives of Aḥmad Shah, who died in his Paris exile in 1930; the name reappeared in France in February 2015 when Renault announced the launch of a new car called Kadjar, causing some kerfuffle among family members.[5]

Many descendants of Fatḥ-'Ali Shah coined surnames using the old *nasab* form, connecting themselves to individual ancestors. Some, such as the Firuz family, named after 'Abbās Mirzā's son Firuz Mirzā Noṣrat al-Dowleh, followed the letter of the 1925 law by choosing a first name. The descendants of another son of 'Abbās Mirzā, Farhād Mirzā Mo'tamed al-Dowleh, chose to name themselves Farhād Mo'tamed.[6] Others added the relative *-i*, such as the descendants of Mas'ud Mirzā Ẓell al-Solṭān, who called themselves Mas'udi. In an unusual case of matrilineality, Nāṣer al-Din Shah's youngest brother, 'Abd al-Ṣamad Mirzā 'Ezz al-Dowleh, and his two sons, Qahramān Mirzā 'Eyn al-Salṭaneh and Ḥoseyn-Qoli Mirzā 'Emād al-Salṭaneh, chose Sālur, this being the Turkoman tribe to which 'Ezz al-Dowleh's mother had belonged.[7]

3. Wipert v. Blücher, *Zeitenwende in Iran: Erlebnisse und Beobachtungen* (Biberach an der Riss: Koehler & Voigtländer, 1949), 218. It should be noted that many historians consider Blücher's account untrustworthy.

4. Niyāzmand, *Reżā Shāh*, 45–46.

5. The Renault Kadjar is based on the vehicle platform of the Nissan Qashqai, which is named after an Iranian tribe. Add to that the Japanese automaker Mazda, named after, inter alia, the supreme Zoroastrian deity, and one might be forgiven for suspecting that a certain persophilia pervades the imaginary of Japanese car manufacturers. Cf. *Wikipédia*, s.v. "Kadjar," "Qashqai," and "Mazda": https://fr.wikipedia.org/wiki/Renault_Kadjar, https://fr.wikipedia.org/wiki/Nissan_Qashqai, and https://fr.wikipedia.org/wiki/Mazda_%28automobiles%29, all accessed on 3 December 2016.

6. Massumeh Farhad, personal e-mail communication, 19 July 2015.

7. Maryam Salour, personal e-mail communication, 19 July 2015.

As for the rest of the population, notwithstanding the three examples given in the legislation discussed in chapter 3, very few Iranians adopted a forename as their surname. Zoroastrians seem to have been somewhat more inclined to do so: in a photo of Zoroastrian leaders sitting in front of Tehran's Zoroastrian temple, the ten identified figures include Mehrabān Shāhpur, Bahman Kay Khosrow, Aflāṭun Shāhrokh, Shariyār Bahrām, Kay Khosrow Shāhrokh, and Khodāraḥm Esfandiyār, a slight majority.[8] One Muslim Iranian who famously chose a first name as his surname was Maḥmud Maḥmud, a historian whose chosen family name had been Pahlavi. When ordered to relinquish that surname after Reżā Pahlavi became shah, he chose his first name as family name in protest.[9] Some men seem to have been so confused about the idea of a surname that they adopted the traditional name of a forebear in its entirety: examples include such family names as Āqā Mirzā Moḥammad 'Ali Shirāzi and Moḥammad Esma'il Seyf-'Ali 'Abbās Ābādi.[10]

But otherwise, on what basis did Iranian men invent their surnames? The family names chosen by most Iranians followed a pattern very like the European pattern, deriving from four categories: patronymical, occupational, local, and descriptive.[11] This was not an act of imitation, however, but derived from the pre-existing naming practices discussed in chapter 2.

A patronymical surname is a family name that expresses a filiation with the father or a more distant progenitor in the male line or an affiliation with an admired or revered person, a type of appellation not unfamiliar to Iranians because of the *nasab* and *nisba* discussed in chapter 2. The simplest way to establish such a connection is by adding an *-i* to the name: the son of Moḥsen becomes Mr. Moḥsen*i*. The ending *-iyān* (a cognate of the homophonous Armenian ending) can have the same function: the descendants of a Farhād become the Farhād*iyān* family. Other words that denote (af)filiation are the aforementioned *-zādeh* (born of), as in Ḥasan Taqi*zādeh*, whose father was indeed known as Seyyed Taqi. Sometimes *-i* and *-zādeh* could be combined, as in Qamar al-Moluk Vazir*izādeh*, the legendary singer who chose her name as an act of homage to 'Ali-Naqi Vaziri, the pioneer of musical modernism in Iran. The suffix *-pur* (son [of]) was another way to signify (af)filiation, as in Sāsān*pur*, which was probably meant to suggest a relation with the Sasanians. It could also be added to another signifier of

8. Monica M. Ringer, *Pious Citizens: Reforming Zoroastrianism in India and Iran* (Syracuse: Syracuse University Press, 2011), 172.

9. Niyāzmand, *Reżā Shāh*, 55–56 n15.

10. "Rāyejtarin va ṭulānitarin nām-e khānevādegi-ye irāni," at http://www.tabnak.ir/fa/pages/?cid=62442. Accessed 28 November 2015.

11. E. C. Smith, *The Story of Our Names* (New York: Harper and Brothers Publishers, 1950), 44. (The author mentions the categories in a different order.)

(af)filiation, as in Moḥtasham*ipur*. A reference to a forefather can also be established by adding *-niyā*, meaning ancestor, to a name. When added to the word *pir* (literally "old," but here meaning "spiritual guide") in Pir 'Abd al-Vahhāb, a venerated Sufi master buried in Nā'in, the result was the surname Pir*niyā*, adopted by two of his descendants, the brothers Mo'tamen al-Molk and Moshir al-Dowleh, both prominent statesmen and literati in late Qājār times.[12] Finally, there is the word *nezhād*, which, like the word "race," originally meant "lineage" but later came to have a phenotypical meaning. *Nezhād* could be added to a name, as in Akbar*nezhād* (of the lineage of Akbar), or to a human aggregate, as in the case of the somewhat eclectically named 1950s athlete Moḥammad Āryā*nezhād* (Moḥammad of the race of the Aryans).[13]

The egalitarian animus of the legislators who gave Iranians surnames notwithstanding, the simple *-i* (or *-iyān*) was also used to perpetuate social distinction. Tribal leaders adopted family names featuring the name of their tribe, such as Afshāri, Bakhtiyāri, or Qashqā'i, either alone or in conjunction with another name. *Seyyeds*, i.e. people claiming descent from the Prophet Muḥammad through his daughter Faṭima, often appended the *-i* or *-iyān* to the name or title of the last of the (Twelver) Imams from whom they descended: 'Alavi, Mortażavi, and Torābi for the first Imam, 'Ali ibn Abi Ṭāleb; Ṭabāṭabā'i and Mojtabavi for the second Imam, Ḥasan ibn 'Ali; Ḥoseyni for the third Imam, Ḥoseyn ibn 'Ali; Sajjādi for the fourth Imam, 'Ali ibn Ḥoseyn Zeyn al-'Ābedin; Bāqeri for the fifth Imam, Moḥammad al-Bāqer; Ṣādeqi and Ja'fari for the sixth Imam, Ja'far al-Ṣādeq; Musavi and Kāẓemi for the seventh Imam, Musā al-Kāẓem; Rażavi for the eighth Imam, 'Ali ibn Musā al-Reżā; Taqavi for the ninth Imam, Moḥammad al-Taqi; Naqavi for the tenth Imam, 'Ali al-Naqi; and 'Askari for the eleventh Imam, Ḥasan al-'Askari (the twelfth of the Twelver Imams left no offspring). Abṭaḥi, Khātami, Moṣṭafavi, and Nabavi are relative adjectives denoting descent from the Prophet Muḥammad and can therefore serve for all *seyyeds*.[14] (Some disagreement seems to persist as to the significance of the name Ṭabāṭabā'i. For some, it refers to *seyyeds* who claim descent from both Imam Ḥasan and Imam Ḥoseyn, the daughter of the latter having married the former's son. For others, it indicates that both one's parents were *seyyeds*. For his part, the scholar Moḥammad Moḥiṭ Ṭabāṭabā'i asserted that only *seyyeds* who were

12. Moḥammad Ebrāhim Bāstāni Pārizi, *Talāsh-e āzādi* (Tehran: Enteshārāt-e Khorram, 1379/2000), 43.

13. *Niru va Rāsti*, 303, 28 Tir 1329 / 19 July 1950, 6.

14. I thank Professor Aḥmad Mahdavi Dāmghāni for this list.

descended from Ibrahim Ṭabāṭabā, a great-grandson of Imam Ḥasan, were entitled to call themselves Ṭabāṭabā'i.[15]

After the abolition of the honorary titles, many members of the elite perpetuated their memory by adding *-i* to the first element of their (or a famous ancestor's) title; thus, the descendants of Amin al-Dowleh (Confidant of the State) became Amini. Others did without the *-i*: the statesmen Vos̱uq al-Dowleh and Qavām al-Salṭaneh (Support of the Monarchy), brothers who were each prime minister a number of times, took the surnames Vos̱uq and Qavām, respectively. Still others let themselves be inspired by their title: 'Adl al-Molk (Justice of the Realm) became Dādgar ("dispenser of justice" in Persian). This tendency was occasionally criticized as being contrary to the spirit of the reforms. Aḥmad Kasravi, the maverick modernist ideologue and historian of the Constitutional Revolution who was assassinated in 1946 because of alleged apostasy, was unhappy with the outcome of the onomastic reforms. Surnames, he wrote, were repetitive, meaningless words, and many people had shortened their titles to generate a family name.[16] The journalist and politician 'Ali Dashti condemned this practice in one of his essays from prison, where he wrote:

> I do not think the Iranian people can let go of *ta'ārof*;[17] they can perhaps renounce their religion, but *ta'ārof* and hollow protestations of friendship are part of their nature. A few years ago titles were abolished by law, but in private circles they have remained alive and commonly used. Some took the first word of their title and used it as their surname so as to keep at least half their title and bequeath to their descendants the honor that they had paid 100 ashrafis to acquire.[18]

Another way in which traditional nomenclature generated surnames was when poets chose their pen name, their *takhalloṣ*, as their family name. This was the case of the two poets laureate Ṣabā and Bahār.

Merchants and artisans adopted occupational surnames. Merchants

15. Moḥammad Moḥiṭ Ṭabāṭabā'i, "Shukhi va jeddi," *Yaghmā* 18:1 (1344/1965–66), 42. According to some sources, this Ibrāhim Ṭabāṭabā had a peculiar way of speaking, which is what earned him the onomatopoeic epithet Ṭabāṭabā.

16. Aḥmad Kasravi, *Khᵛāharān va dokhtarān-e mā* (1944, Bethesda, MD: Iranbooks, 1371/1992), 80.

17. *Ta'ārof* is an untranslatable staple of Iranian social life. It refers to a ritual (and, if taken literally, most often insincere) exchange of polite formulas. For a discussion, see William O. Beeman, *Language, Status, and Power in Iran* (Bloomington: Indiana University Press, 1986), 139–162.

18. 'Ali Dashti, "Ta'ārof va dorugh," in *Ayyām-e maḥbas* (Tehran: Enteshārāt-e Asāṭir, 1380/2001), 224. The essay is dated 13 Mordād 1312 / 4 August 1933.

often used the Arabic designation for their profession, such as Razzāz (rice-seller), or added the Turkish suffix *-chi*[19] to the wares they traded in, e.g. Jurāb*chi* (trader in hosiery).[20] A suffix denoting the plural might be added to the *-chi*, as in Farsh*chiyān* (carpet dealer[s]). The shortened agent noun form of a verb might also be added, most often *-forush* (seller), as in Bolur*forush* (seller of crystalware). A few merchants took surnames ending in the suffix *-iyeh* (which is somewhat reminiscent of royal or spiritual dynasties), such as Qāsemiyeh. Artisans often just took their trade designation, such as Dabbāgh (tanner) or Qannād (confectioner). Alternatively, they might add the appropriate shortened agent noun to the name of whatever they produced. Examples are *-afkan* (thrower), as in Tir*afkan* (thrower of spears); *-bāf* (weaver), as in Qāli*bāf* (carpet weaver); *-duz* (sewer or embroiderer), as in Zar*duz* (gold sewer = embroiderer); *-riz* (scatterer), as in Gol*riz* (scatterer of flowers); and *-sāz* (maker), as in Chit*sāz* (maker of chintz). The ending *-i* or *-iyān* could also be added to these occupational designations, yielding surnames such as Ḥajjār*iyān* (stonecutter) or Chāy*chiyān* (tea dealer). Agentive suffixes like *-gar*, *-gār*, and *-kār* could be added to a noun to indicate a connection with the signified of the noun, as in Tavān*gar* (well-to-do), Āmuze*gār* (teacher), and Nāzok*kār* (detailer, mostly in masonry).[21] On the shores of the Persian Gulf, finally, surnames such as Ṣayyād and Māhigir (fisherman) appeared, as well as surnames containing the word *daryā* ("sea" in Iranian Persian).

Surnames pointing to a connection with places were nothing but petrified demonyms (*nisbas*). They could refer to a village, as in Kani; a town or city, as in Tabrizi; an urban quarter, as in Sangelaji; a district, as in Shemirāni; or a province, as in Khorāsāni. Places in neighboring lands could yield family names as well, such as ʿĀmeli (from Jabal ʿAmel in today's Lebanon), Ḥejāzi or Makki (Meccan). The shrine cities of Iraq generated Gharavi, Kāzemeyni, and Ḥā'eri, indicating connections with Najaf, Kazemeyn, and Karbala, respectively. This kind of toponymic *nisba* was often added to the initial surname to distinguish between unrelated extended families that had adopted

19. In the Turkish of Turkey, *-chi* becomes *-cu*, *-çu*, *-cü*, *-çü*, *-ci*, *-çi*, *-cı*, or *-çı*, depending on the requirements of vowel harmony. In Turkish and Persian this suffix has the same function as *walla* in India.

20. According to the amateur social historian of Tehran Jaʿfar Shahri, however, men who were known by names ending with *chi* or *bāshi* were generally disliked by the populace for being unkind and ungrateful, and people admonished their children to stay away from them: *Gushehhā'i az tārikh-e ejtemāʿi-ye Tehrān-e qadim* (Tehran: Moʿin, 1370/1991), 163. He gives no explanation or reason for this.

21. Abdolmajid Memar-Sadeghi, "Changing Personal Names and Titles in Written Farsi, 1921–1978: A Sociolinguistic Study with Pedagogical Implications" (PhD Thesis, University of Illinois at Urbana-Champaign, 1980), 118–119, 173, and 194.

the same family name,[22] but interestingly enough, a family carrying such a demonym often did not live in the eponymous city, the *nisba* having been added when they moved from their original home to a new city, in an effort to differentiate them from those bearers of the surname who were natives of that city.[23] Family names could also express an ethnic or tribal group affiliation, as in 'Arab, Tork, or Baluch.

Descriptive surnames in Iran tended to be aspirational, perhaps reflecting the oft-noted preference of Iranians for idealism over realism. Many Iranians took a desirable concept and added another word to it, with the resulting compound signifying their moral aspirations. Such words were often agent nouns shorn of their *-andeh* ending, which left in effect the verbal stem. Examples are *-andish* (thinker [about]), *-ārā* (embellisher [of]), *-āvar* (bringer [of]), *-bakhsh* (giver [of]), *-bar* (carrier [of]), *-bin* (seer), *-dār* (possessor [of]), *-dust* (lover or friend [of]), *-gu* (sayer [of]), *-ju* (seeker [of]), *-kh^{v}āh* (seeker [of]), *-panāh* ([giver of] refuge [to]), and *-parast* (worshipper [of]). Thus, when a devout Muslim in Kermanshah wanted his surname to allude to his religious beliefs and proposed the names Towḥidi (monotheistic), Nabavi (pertaining to the Prophet), 'Edālatkh^{v}āh (seeker of justice), Emāmi (pertaining to the Imam), and Ma'ādi (pertaining to the Resurrection), the registry official told him that all these surnames had already been taken. So they compromised by adding the suffix *-kh^v*āh to Ma'ādi, yielding Ma'ādikh^{v}āh,[24] which does not make much sense grammatically or semantically.

The second elements in such compounds were not always verbal stems like *-kh^v*āh; we also find *-bakht* (luck), *-fām* (hue), *far* (holder or splendor [of]), *-kār* (cultivator [of]), *-kish* (believer [in]), *-mand* (partaker [of]), *-manesh* ([having the] manner [of]), *-nām* (name), *-vand* (affiliated [with]), and *-yār* (friend [of]). The words to which these elements were added expressed the ideals of those who coined the names. These ideals could be moral, as in the many surnames that contain the words *'adl*, *dād*, *'edālat* (all meaning justice), and 'ādel (just); religious, as in the many surnames containing *eslām* and *din* (religion); or patriotic, as in the many surnames containing the nouns *Irān*, *Pārs*, and *Āryā*.[25] Among elite families, such names are considered *esm-e bi-*

22. This becomes especially important when two people have identical first and family names: to wit, Iraj Afshār Yazdi and Iraj Afshār Sistāni, both scholars in Iranian studies.

23. In my own extended family, for example, it is those from Mashhad whose full surname is Shahābi Sirjāni.

24. As told in the memoirs of his son: Ḥojjat al-Eslām 'Abd al-Majid Ma'ādikh^{v}āh, *Jām-e shekasteh: Khāṭerāt* (Tehran: Markaz-e Asnād-e Enqelāb-e Eslāmi, 1382/2003), 51.

25. For the origin of the Iranians' infatuation with Aryanness, see David Motadel, "Iran and the Aryan myth," in Ali M. Ansari, ed., *Perceptions of Iran: History, Myths and Nationalism from Medieval Persia to the Islamic Republic* (London: I.B. Tauris, 2014), 119–145.

mosammā, "names without a referent," for which reason they are sometimes derided as *man darāvardi*, "made up by myself," i.e., self-coined names that do not refer to any family antecedent, the implication being that the family has no ancestor worthy of being proud of.

Non-Muslim names could sometimes be recognized at first sight, but not always. Armenian surnames almost invariably end in *iyān* or *iyānts*, but many Muslims, Jews, and Baha'is have surnames ending in *iyān* as well.

Zoroastrians tended to choose old Persian names as the raw material for their surnames, but at times they also used words of Arabic origin. In the village of Qāsemābād, near Yazd, the resident Zoroastrian farmers took the name Zāre', which means "farmer" in Arabic. When there were too many Zāre's, some added Zardoshti (Zoroastrian) to their surname. But soon there were too many Zāre'-e Zardoshtis, so one man added yet a third element to this family name, which became Zāre'-e Zardoshti-ye Tandari.[26]

Jews generally chose surnames similar or analogous to those of Muslims. Merchants and artisans used their professional designations, such as Abrishami (Silk maker), Almāsi (Diamond dealer), Boluriyān (Crystal maker), Javāheriyān (jeweler), or Zargar (goldsmith), some adding *-chi*, such as Abrisham*chi* (Merchant of silk), Sā'at*chi* (Watch seller), or 'Araq*chi* (Merchant of alcoholic drinks). When surnames referred to an ancestor or a religious figure, they were constructed along the same principles as Muslim ones, except that the referents were taken from the Jewish religious tradition: Shā'ul*i* (related to Saul), Elqān*iyān* (related to Elkan), Soleymān*zādeh* (son of Solomon), Esḥāq*pur* (son of Isaac), or Dāvud*nezhād* (from the race of David). Levites and Kohanim coined surnames such as Levi, Lāvi, Lavā'i, Lāvizādeh, Lavā'iyān, Kohan, Kohanpur, etc. In a number of places, including Isfahan, the registry officials also automatically inserted the noun Kalimi ("Jewish," deriving from the title of Moses, Kalim Allāh, in the Islamic tradition; see above) in every Jew's name.[27]

The cosmopolitan quest of the Baha'is for the unity of all human beings drove many to choose surnames based on words containing the trilateral Arabic root w (pronounced v in Persian) - ḥ - d, on which the words for unity, oneness, alliance, and ally are based: examples include Vaḥdat, Vaḥdati, Vaḥidi, Vāḥedi, and Vāḥediān. Baha'i merchants from around the country who were not related by blood ties but established commercial partnerships together chose names like Mottaḥedin, Mottaḥedeh, Etteḥādiyeh, and

26. Personal telephone communication from the man's grandson, Fariborz Zareh, 6 March 2016.

27. Doktor 'Abd al-Karim Behniyā, *Nām: pazhuheshi dar nāmhā-ye irāniyān-e mo'āṣer* (Tehran: Enteshārāt-e Shahid Farhād Reżā, 1360/1981, 1374/1995), 35–36.

Shorakā – although not all who adopted these names were Baha'is. After the break between 'Abd al-Bahā, the Prophet Baha'ullah's son and successor, and his brother Moḥammad 'Ali, many of the Baha'is who remained loyal to 'Abd al-Bahā chose names that referred to the strength of the covenant they had with him: Rāsekh (Steadfast), S̱ābet (Firm), Peymān (Covenant), and 'Ahdiyeh (pertaining to a covenant) come to mind.[28]

Finally, in Baluchistan, formerly enslaved Afro-Iranians celebrated their emancipation in 1929 by adopting surnames such as Shanbeh Āzādi (Freedom Saturday), Jom'eh Āzādi (Freedom Friday), and Chahārshanbeh Āzādi (Freedom Wednesday).[29]

In rural areas, registry agents suggested names for those who could not think of one themselves. In one case a villager was asked what he did. His answer was: *zaḥmat mikasham*, "I toil." So he was given the surname Zaḥmatkash, "Toiler."[30] But the derivation of a name is not always this transparent. In the village of Sedeh, near Isfahan, a merchant regularly called to buy the inhabitants' handmade objects, which were locally known as *kār* (work), to sell them in the city. When he had to adopt a surname, the official suggested *Kārkherān*, the verb *kharidan* (to buy) being pronounced *kheridan* in Isfahan. But in Tehran the name was pronounced *Kārkharān*, suggesting not only a connection with commercial activity but also with *khar*, donkey. The man's sons therefore obtained permission to insert a *yā* into their name, so that as *Kārkheyrān* their family name would suggest good works (*kheyr* = good).[31]

Rural folk sometimes refused to meet with the registry official visiting their village, and the representatives of the state sometimes retaliated by assigning them ridiculous names. An amateur onomastician reports having come across surnames such as Sag koshteh khar khordeh zamin (Slew dog, donkey has fallen), Cheheltokhmeh (Forty-seeded or -testicled), Māhgerefteh (a reference to a birthmark), and Ātashgerefteh (Aflame). Occasionally a registrar would make a spelling mistake or write illegibly. When a school principal complained to the registry that his pupils' names were illegible, an exasperated registrar told him not to try to figure out what the name

28. Mehrdad Amanat, personal telephone communication, 10 March 2015.

29. Maḥmud Zand Moqaddam, *Ḥekāyat-e Baluch*, volume 2: *Kordhā, Englishā, Baluchhā* (Tehran: Published by the author, 1371/1992), 441–442. For a discussion of slavery in Iran see Behnaz A. Mirzai, "African Presence in Iran: Identity and Its Reconstruction in the 19th and 20th Centuries," *Revue Française d'Histoire d'Outremer* 89, Nos. 336–337 (2002): 229–246.

30. Fatema Soudavar, personal e-mail communication, 31 August 2015.

31. His granddaughter became a lawyer and dropped the *kheyrān* in her professional life, becoming known as *Mehrangiz Kār*. Mehranguiz Kar, personal communication, Cambridge, Mass., 12 November 2015.

actually was but just to reproduce the shape of the name.[32] In Ardabil, a peddler who brought wares from town to sell in the surrounding villages could not think of a name, and so he was given the name Khar-e Ṣaḥrā'i (Desert Donkey).[33] Nor did such names always belong to unfortunate peasants: when the mansion of one of Kermanshah's leading families was looted and destroyed in the course of the revolt of Prince Sālār al-Dowleh, and all family documents were lost, the family chose the surname Khānehkharāb ([Of a] Ruined House).[34]

The initial idea, so often voiced by the earliest owners of family names in the early 1920s, that those who had taken a name first had an exclusive right to it, could not be enforced in the long run. And so, when one surname became too common, the original bearers of it would sometimes add Moqaddam (Having Precedence), Fard (Unique, the Main One), or Aṣl (Original) to their family name to indicate their superior claim to it.[35] Even if a person was not the original bearer of the name, he would sometimes change it simply because too many other people were carrying it, to wit this advertisement, where a Dr. Emāmi requests his friends and patients to call him Seyyed Emāmi because there were too many people carrying the name Emāmi (Figure 13):[36]

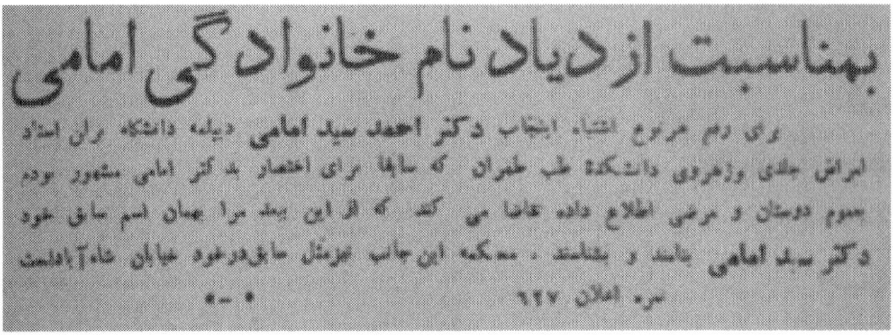
بمناسبت ازدیاد نام خانوادگی امامی

برای رفع مرجوع اشتباه، اینجانب دکتر احمد سید امامی دیپلمه دانشگاه برلن استاد امراض جلدی و زهروی دانشکدهٔ طب طهران که سالها برای اختصار به دکتر امامی مشهور بودم بعموم دوستان و مرضی اطلاع داده تقاضا می کند که از این ببعد مرا بهمان اسم سابق خود دکتر سید امامی بنامند و بشناسند. مطب اینجانب در منزل سابق خود خیابان شاه‌آباد است

نمره اعلان ۶۲۷

Figure 13: Name change

32. Behniyā, *Nām*, 37–38.

33. Bābā Safari, *Ardabil dar goẕargāh-e tārikh*, volume 2 (Ardabil: Islamic Azad University Press, 1991), 9.

34. Moḥammad 'Ali Solṭāni, *Tārikh-e mofaṣṣal-e Kermānshāhān*, volume 4 (Tehran: Moḥammad 'Ali Solṭāni, 1373/1994), 1139. For the activities of the prince see Reżā Āẕari, ed., *Dar takāpu-ye tāj va takht: Asnād-e Abu al-Fatḥ Mirzā Sālār al-Dowleh Qājār* (Tehran: Enteshārāt-e Sāzmān-e Asnād-e Melli-ye Irān, 1378/1999).

35. Bābā Safari, *Ardabil dar goẕargāh-e tārikh*, volume 2, 9. The author's forenames are nowhere indicated on the book cover – not a unique case.

36. *Eṭṭelā'āt*, 11 Ordibehesht 1316 / 1 May 1937, 8.

The fact that men chose their surnames meant that at times brothers would acquire different ones. Ruḥ Allāh Khomeini's surname was registered as Moṣṭafavi in Golpāyegān because his father's name was Moṣṭafā. But when an official went to Khomeyn to register his brothers' names, they were not allowed to take Moṣṭafavi on account of it having already been taken, so the two younger brothers chose Hendi ("Indian," because their grandfather had emigrated to India); soon, however, they were told to change it because it suggested ties to Britain. So the middle brother changed his surname to Pasandideh, but the youngest kept Hendi. Thus three brothers ended up with three different family names.[37]

As this brief survey shows, Iranians used a wide variety of sources to coin surnames. As elsewhere in the world, some became more common than others. By 2016 the most common family names throughout the country were Mohammadi, Musavi, Aḥmadi, Karimi, and Ja'fari, in that order.[38]

One puzzling feature of Iranian naming conventions is the insertion of an *eżāfeh* (the enclitic *-e*) between the forename and the surname in spoken Persian.[39] In the absence of sound recordings of the parliamentary debates of the 1920s, it is impossible to say whether in their debates the legislators connected Eskandar to Ebrāhim, Iraj to Kāvus, and Maḥmud to Kāmrān in this way, since the *eżāfeh* is a short vowel and therefore not written out. One might hypothesize that since an *eżāfeh* was customary for traditional *nisbas* and *nasabs*, e.g. Hātef-e Eṣfahāni and Ardeshir-e Bābakan, it was also automatically adopted in the case of surnames ending in the relative-*i* and *-zādeh*, after which the practice was generalized. Exceptions exist: forenames ending with long vowels or Allāh are as a rule not connected to the surname with an *eżāfeh* in spoken Persian, e.g. Reżā Pahlavi, Nimā Yushij, Leylā Khātami, 'Abd Allāh Mostowfi, Khosrow Shākeri, and Holāku Rāmbod (but cf. Khāju-ye Kermāni).

Family Names in the Social Context

In the immediate aftermath of the 1925 reforms, there was some confusion, as had happened with such reforms elsewhere.[40] The post office first announced that letters featuring only titles would not be delivered, but then

37. As recounted in the reminiscences of Ayatollah Pasandideh: Moḥammad Javād Morādiniyā, ed. *Khāṭerāt-e Āyat Allāh Pasandideh* (Enteshārāt-e Ḥadis̱, 1374/1995), 50 and 53–54.

38. http://www.rajanews.com/news/82221. Accessed 20 July 2017.

39. For an explanation of this feature of the Persian language see *Encyclopaedia Iranica*, s.v. "eżāfa" (by John R. Perry and Ali Ashraf Sadeghi).

40. For the case of Japan see Herbert Plutschow, *Japan's Name Culture: The Significance of Names in a Religious, Political and Social Context* (Sandgate: Japan Library, 1995), 193–194.

relented. The new rules added to the workload of mailmen, telegraph officials, and office employees, as they now had to track down people who were using the new names and figure out which new names corresponded to which old ones.[41]

We have already seen that after the passage of the 1925 law establishing a nationwide civil status registry, some of the registry personnel took advantage of peasants who were ignorant of their age by threatening to record a year of birth that would make them liable to be drafted. There were other worries too. In Khomeyn, we learn from the memoirs of Ayatollah Khomeini's brother, Ayatollah Pasandideh that when an official came to the town to register people's names, there was resistance to his attempt to get men to reveal the names of their wives and mothers, and petitions and telegrams were sent to Tehran to protest against his work.[42] In Ardabil, the arrival of the registry in 1928 generated some anxiety, and all sorts of rumors started circulating among the common people. The inhabitants usually bought a year's worth of wheat at harvest time and then stored the flour at home, and rumor had it that the registry was meant to ration bread, as well as to take young men away to do military service. The second was true, of course, as we have seen, and therefore many young men grew long beards and shaved their heads to appear older, hoping to persuade the registrars that they were too old to be drafted. When the day of the draft arrived, in the autumn of 1928, the army tried to lighten the mood by having the regimental brass band play joyful tunes.[43] The centralizing measures of the state also met with resistance from the tribes, which resented the intrusion of the tentacles of the state into their affairs. In 1928 the Qashqa'is of Fars province rebelled, battling government forces for over a year.[44] Their grievances included conscription and the oppressive presence of civil registry officials.[45]

The establishment of state registries for matters of personal status was a blow to the Shiite ulema, whose work was now subordinated to the state, just as in France after 1792 the state curtailed the role of the Roman Catholic clergy. Although they themselves were exempted from military

41. Qahramān Mirzā Sālur, 'Eyn al-Salṭaneh, *Ruznāmeh-ye khāṭerāt-e 'Eyn al-Salṭaneh (Qahramān Mirzā)*, ed. Mas'ud Sālur and Iraj Afshār, volume 9 (Tehran: Asāṭir, 1379/2000), 7324–7325.

42. Morādiniyā, ed., *Khāṭerāt-e Āyat Allāh Pasandideh*, 86.

43. Bābā Safari, *Ardabil dar gozargāh-e tārikh*, volume 2, 8–9.

44. Pierre Oberling, *The Qashqā'i Nomads of Fārs* (The Hague: Mouton, 1974), 149–167; and Kāveh Bayāt, *Shuresh-e 'ashāyeri-ye* Fārs: sālhā-ye 1307-*1309 H.Sh.* (Tehran: Nashr-e Noqreh, bā hamkāri-ye Enteshārāt-e Zarrin, 1365/1986).

45. Bāqer 'Āqeli, *Ruzshomār-e tārikh-e Irān az mashruṭeh tā enqelāb-e eslāmi* (Tehran: Nashr-e Goftār, 1369/1990), 169.

service, a number of ulema issued fatwas against conscription.[46] In Isfahan, for instance, some clerics suggested that the state wanted to expose young men to immoral behavior, illnesses such as gonorrhea and syphilis, and homosexuality.[47]

The modern educational system and the reformed judiciary had already marginalized the Shiite clergy; then, in 1932 registries of deeds were established. This further eroded the social role of the ulema, who had traditionally recorded transactions and contracts. Many responded by opening secular registration offices (*maḥżar*), thereby consenting to become state-regulated notaries public.[48] Rabbis also registered as *maḥżardār*s to cater to the needs of the Jewish communities.[49]

In the end, however, the abolition of titles and the introduction of family names and identity cards was accepted by Iranians, like many other state- and nation-building reforms of the Reżā Shah period. While given names have been subject to periodic waves of fashion dictated by the dominant political culture (or the reaction against it),[50] surnames have remained largely stable, except that after the revolution of 1979 some Iranians whose family names contained the word *shāh* changed them to escape allegations of royalism. Thus a Mr. Shāhdusti became Eslāmdusti, a Mr. Shahbandari became Shahid Bandari, and a Mr. Shahdusti became Dustmadāri.[51]

Surnames have come to be taken for granted, and almost all Iranians use a forename and a family name for official purposes, each of which can consist of two (or sometimes even three) elements, as illustrated above. In fact, the use of family names caught on to such an extent that until recently,

46. Mehdi Farrokh, *Khāṭerāt-e siyāsi-ye Farrokh, Moʿtaṣem al-Salṭaneh* (Tehran: Sāzmān-e Enteshārāt-e Jāvidān, n.d.), 223.

47. Markaz-e Asnād-e Enqelāb-e Eslāmi, ed., *Haftād sāl khāṭereh az Āyat a... Seyyed Ḥoseyn Bodalā* (Tehran: Markaz-e Asnād-e Enqelāb-e Eslāmi, 1378/1999), 107–110.

48. Aḥmad Mahdavi Dāmghāni, "Tārikhcheh-ye maḥżar va daftar-e asnād-e rasmi," *Bokhārā* 89–90 (Mehr–Dey 1391 / September–December 2002), 122–137.

49. Homa Sarshar, personal e-mail communication, 8 November 2015.

50. Franciszek Machalski, "Die Personennamen der Schuljugend von Iran," *Folia Orientalia* 12 (1970): 155–163; Nader Habibi, "Iranian Names," *International Journal of Middle East Studies* 24:2 (May 1992): 253–260; Eḥsān Yārshāter, "Nāmhā-ye irāni," *Irānshenāsi* 1:2 (Summer 1368/1989): 324–329; Doktor Aḥmad Rajabzādeh, *Taḥlil-e ejtemāʿi-ye nāmgoẕāri* (Tehran: Ravesh, 1378/1999). In Turkey, too, the frequency of different forenames has changed with the vagaries of secularization. See Richard W. Bulliet, "First Names and Political Change in Modern Turkey," *International Journal of Middle East Studies* 9:4 (November 1978): 489–495; Ilhan Başgöz, "The Meaning and Dimension of Change in Personal Names in Turkey," *Turcica* 15 (1983): 201–218; Annemarie Schimmel, *Herr "Demirci" heißt einfach "Schmidt": Türkische Namen und ihre Bedeutung* (Cologne: Önel-Verlag, 1992), 6–45; and Spencer, "The Social Context": 212–217.

51. "Taghyir-e asāmi-ye khānevādegi az nowʿ-e ṭaghuti beh nowʿ-e eslāmi," *Iran Times*, 21 May 1982, 13.

schoolchildren routinely called each other by their surnames, a practice also attested in schools elsewhere in the world. But their use also had class dimensions: the surnames of middle- and upper-class people were used more often in actual social interactions than were those of lower-class people, and the surnames of domestic servants were rarely even known to their employers, who called the maid or the valet by their first names.[52] As the author of a doctoral dissertation on names put it:

> As a native speaker of Farsi the researcher is quite aware of the fact that when somebody's [first name] is heard even now ... among many of the older speech communities, the impression a Persian speaker has is that the reference is to an immature young person, a servant, a janitor, or a member of a low class of the country.[53]

One interesting phenomenon that deserves further attention is the fact that married women tend to keep their maiden names for public identification, even though, as we have seen, according to the law they must take that of their husband upon marrying. This is not as counterintuitive as it seems, as the custom of a woman exchanging her father's surname for her husband's is a relatively recent phenomenon even in Europe and the retention of the father's name is actually a hallmark of patriarchy.[54]

By the same token, many modern women often referred to their husband by his surname – unless they called him *Doktor*, *Mohandes* (engineer) or *Timsār* (an honorific used for officers above the rank of colonel). Actual use of the family name was something of a status symbol, as could be seen in the hugely popular television and cinema series based on the village character Ṣamad, in which another villager with pretensions of upward mobility, named 'Eyn Allāh, constantly asks to be called by his family name, Bāqerzādeh. Actors and singers often use only one name, which for either men or women might be a forename (Dāriush, Hāydeh, Benyāmin), or, in the case of men only, could be a surname (e.g. the immortal comic trio of prerevolutionary Iranian cinema: Sepehrniyā, Garshā, and Motevasselāni).[55]

52. I have mentioned my own experience with this in the introduction. Drivers seem to have been the exception and were often addressed by their surname, perhaps because their profession implied the mastery of modern skills – after all, their professional designation was *shofor*, from the French *chauffeur*.

53. Memar-Sadeghi, "Changing Personal Names," 105–106.

54. "Eusebius Salverte" [Anne Joseph Eusèbe Baconnière Salverte], *History of the Names of Men, Nations, and Places in their Connection with the Progress of Civilization*, trans. L.H. Mordacque (London: John Russell Smith, 1862), 250.

55. The use of mononyms is of course not specific to Iranian entertainers: think of Dalida, Adamo, Donovan, Madonna, and Heino, to take examples from France, Belgium/Italy, Britain, the United States, and Germany, respectively. The Italo-Belgian singer (Salvatore) Adamo, incidentally, whose 1967 hit song *Inch'Allah* made him known in Iran, was given the (nonheredi-

Since the revolution of 1979, when men who hailed from the provinces, and whose surnames made that clear, started dominating the political and social scene (Khomeyn, Rafsanjān, Khāmeheh, are all places outside Tehran), some people have taken to adding a place-*nisba* to their names, presumably to signify that they are rooted in the "true," "authentic" Iran. Only among religious figures does a certain ambivalence concerning surnames seem to linger, as reflected in the fact that many are known by names other than the ones that have been registered for them. Ayatollah Borujerdi signed his fatwas Ṭabaṭābā'i, and Ayatollah Khomeini's registered surname (as we have seen) was Moṣṭafavi (also used by his daughters but not by his sons);[56] 'Ali Shari'ati's official surname was Mazināni, Navvāb Ṣafavi was the nom de guerre of Mojtabā Mirlowḥi, Ṣādeq Khalkhāli's family name was Ṣādeqi Givi, and 'Ali Akbar Hāshemi Rafsanjāni's was Bahramāni, while 'Ali Akbar Moḥtashami's is Moḥtashamipur and 'Abd al-Karim Sorush's full name is Ḥoseyn Ḥājj Karim Dabbāgh. Of the fifty-one clerical Shiite members of the Assembly of Experts that finalized the constitution of the Islamic Republic in 1979, sixteen used a different name than the one in their identity card. (So, incidentally, did the Jewish member of the assembly.)[57] One wonders whether this indifference to the state's role in fixing a name stems from a lingering antipathy to the state's interference in people's lives, or whether the fact that in 1919 and 1926 the government allowed clerics not to go the registry in person is what has led to this discrepancy. Another reason is that in Najaf, where many Shiite ulema studied, family names were not used. One cleric remembers that when he arrived in the shrine city in 1953, the first thing he was asked was where he was from. When he answered that he was from Zanjān, his interlocutors would point out that there are many Zanjānis and would ask whether he was from the city itself. Upon being told that he was from the village of Kho'eyn, they would tell him that thenceforth he would be called Mr. Kho'eyni. He adds:

tary) title of *chevalier* (knight) by King Albert II of the Belgians in 2001, a belated confirmation that titles are not incompatible with a modern society, a point made by Moḥammad Vali Mirzā in 1925 (see above). (One might add that the Belgian constitution is still in force after more than a hundred and seventy years, whereas the Iranian one inspired by it lasted only just over sixty years.)

56. This discrepancy may have had a major effect on world history: When Ayatollah Khomeini was compelled to leave Najaf in the autumn of 1978, the passport in which he received a Kuwaiti visa was in the name of Ruḥollāh Moṣṭafavi. When the Kuwaiti authorities at the border realized who he was, they refused to let him in, whereupon he went to Paris. Baqer Moin, *Khomeini: Life of the Ayatollah* (London: I.B. Tauris, 2009), p. 189.

57. *Rāhnamā-ye estefādeh az ṣurat-e mashruḥ-e mozākerāt-e majles-e barrasi-ye nahā'i-ye qānun-e asāsi-ye jomhuri-ye eslāmi-ye Irān* (Tehran: Edāreh-ye koll-e omur-e farhangi va ravābeṭ-e 'omumi-ye majles-e shurā-ye eslāmi, 1368/1989), 334–405.

> In the seminaries of Najaf they did not care about family names. This turned out to be a divine blessing [literally: act of God's kindness], because when I returned to Iran, I came to be known as Āl-e Esḥāq. For this reason SAVAK did not find me, and two or three other persons were arrested instead of me, such as Ā[qā] Sheykh 'Ali Kho'eyni. In Najaf they tried, as far as possible, to call people by their birthplace. This was an old tradition, as ulema such as Ā[qā] Seyyed Abolḥasan Eṣfahāni and Ayatollah Borujerdi had been known by the places [where they were from], but in Qom it was not like that and people were known by their family names.[58]

The generalization of family names did not, however, lead to the immediate demise of titles; far from it. Within families, titled members were routinely referred to by their titles. After the fall of Reżā Shah, a few statesmen, probably to distance themselves from his regime by showing that since he had not bestowed the title it was not for him to take it away, began using their titles again.[59] The most prominent of these was Qavām al-Salṭaneh,[60] who became prime minister a number of times between 1941 and 1952. But as the bearers of the old titles left this world to meet the One whose shadow had conferred them, the use of titles gradually died out. Most historic figures of the late Qājār era are still commonly referred to by their titles, such as Vos̱uq al-Dowleh, or by a combination of title and surname, such as Ẕokā' al-Molk Forughi. Under the second ruler of the Pahlavi dynasty, the "spirit of the age" was occasionally neglected when a few more titles were given. The poets Qāsem Rasā and Ṣādeq Sarmad were named Malek al-Sho'arā (King of the Poets) of the shrine of Imam Reżā in Mashhad,[61] a title Moḥammad Taqi Bahār had borne, and in 1965 Moḥammad Reżā Shah had himself given the title of *Āryāmehr* (Light/Sun of the Aryans). A general who had changed his name from Abutorābiyān to Āryāmehr in imitation of General Bahrām Āryānā (whose original name was Ḥoseyn Manuchehri) was told to change his name one more time at that point to accommodate the Shah.[62]

After the Constitutional Revolution, the Shiite clerics increasingly used the honorifics *Ḥojjat al-Eslām* and *Āyat Allāh*, perhaps to compensate for their loss of social and political influence. With the prevailing inflation of titles,

58. Moḥammad Reżā Shamsā and Ṭāhereh Mehrvarzān,eds., *Khāṭerāt-e Āyat Allāh 'Ali Āl-e Esḥāq* (Tehran: Enteshārāt-e Markaz-e Asnād-e Enqelāb-e Eslāmi, 1385/2006), 183–184.

59. I owe this insight to Majid Tafreshi.

60. As reflected in the title of a recent book on him and his political party: Ralph Kauz, *Politische Parteien und Bevölkerung in Iran: die Hezb-e Demokrat-e Iran und ihr Führer Qavamo s-Saltana* (Berlin: Klaus Schwarz, 1995).

61. Personal communication, Aḥmad Mahdavi Dāmghāni.

62. Niyāzmand, *Reżā Shāh*, 56 n15.

a new honorific appeared, *Āyat Allāh al-'Oẓmā*, usually translated as Grand Ayatollah.[63] When a biographical dictionary of prominent clerics appeared in the 1970s, the author received many complaints from scholars who did not think that they had been adequately provided with honorifics.[64] More recently, the term *ostād* (master) has been used for people of decreasing professional distinction, inspiring the musician Moḥammad Reżā Loṭfi to use the honorific *ostād-e kāmel* (perfect master) for those musicians he deemed worthy of being thus honored.[65] Such a gradual debasement in terms of address is not uncommon, as seen by the evolution of the use of *monsieur* and *madame* in French. Originally used among the nobility, the terms later came to be used for the general population.[66]

As for the military titles abolished in May 1925, *Sepahbod* reappeared as the grade for a three-star general under Reżā Shah, and *Sardār*, which had been used by Russian officers of the Cossack Brigade,[67] was revived for officers of the Guardians of the Islamic Revolution, the Pāsdārān – the equivalent honorific for regular army officers being *Amir*.

So much for official usage. In informal social interactions, the situation is quite different, and some of the variety that was on display in pre-1925 naming practices, with their *'anāvin* and *alqāb*, still persists. The honorifics abolished in 1935 never completely died out; some linger on in polite society. *Amir* survived by being onomasticized, allowing the last Shah's close friend and confidant and longtime minister of the court, Amir Asad Allāh 'Alam, to get away with continuing to use his ancestral title as heir to the emirs (lords) of Qā'enāt in eastern Iran.[68] Male scions of old landowning families are still sometimes referred to by adding *Khān* to their forenames, and members of the Qājār imperial house still occasionally refer to descendants (through the male line) of Fath-'Ali Shah by adding *Mirzā* to the given name,[69] but it is doubtful that these practices will survive for much longer.

63. Jalāl Matini, "Baḥs̱i darbāreh-ye sābeqeh-ye tārikhi-ye alqāb va 'anavin-e 'olamā dar maẕhab-e shi'eh," *Irānshenāsi* 1:4 (Summer 1983): 588–589.

64. Ḥājj Moḥammad Sharif Rāzi, *Ganjineh-ye dāneshmandān*, volume 2 (Tehran: Ketābforushi-ye Eslāmiyeh, 1352/1973), 312–314.

65. Moḥammad Reża Żiyāyi, "'Ostād' beh cheh kasi miguyand? (Dar bāb-e eghrāq dar alqāb)," *Bokhārā* 109 (Āẕar-Dey 1394/November-December 2015), 364.

66. Herbert Spencer, *The Principles of Sociology*, volume 2 (New Brunswick, NJ: Transaction Publishers, 2002), 175–176.

67. See, for instance, the proclamation signed by Sardār Starosselsky in *Irān*, 16 August 1920, 1.

68. See Pirouz Mojtahed-Zadeh, *The Amirs of the Borderlands and Eastern Iranian Borders* (London: Urosevic Foundation, 1995).

69. Personal observations in fin-de-siècle Tehran and Kerman. The use of *Khān* between forename and family name is somewhat similar to that of *Don* in southern Italy.

In correspondence, *'anāvin* such as *jenāb* (for men) and *sarkār* (for women) are still used, although they too are becoming rarer. One practice outlawed in the 1935 decree, invocatory pious phrases uttered or written after the name of an especially worthy person, made a spectacular comeback in public discourse after the Islamic Revolution, mostly when referring to the ulema or other learned people who were in the ulema's good graces.[70] Another practice introduced after the revolution was to substitute *Barādar* and *Khᵛāhar* (brother and sister) for *Āqā* and *Khānom* (Mr. and Mrs./Miss).

Hājj (unlike in Turkey) and *Seyyed* were never outlawed and have remained in use among the pious, but *Mashhadi* and *Karbalā'i* have become so rare that using them is seen as somewhat tacky. While the modernizers considered titles and honorifics an obstacle to progress, modernization actually led to the appearance of two much-coveted new titles, which certify the bearer as belonging to the educated elite: *doktor* and *mohandes* (engineer).[71] While the use of the former presupposes (at least in theory) that the user possesses a doctorate, the latter is a professional designation given to engineers and architects (and members of technical professions in general) who hold an academic degree below a doctorate. Another way in which Iranians have tried to distinguish themselves is through their signature, which has to be imaginative – meaning, in practice, that most signatures are illegible – so as to be difficult to forge. It also appears that the signatures of important men are bigger than those of lesser souls.[72]

There is one important subgroup of Iran's urban lower and lower-middle classes to whom bynames were absolutely essential: these were the *luṭis*, local toughs who operated on the margins of the law but (at least in theory) adhered to a certain code of chivalry.[73] As the last true representatives of that colorful stratum fade into history, a number of recent studies have endeavored to gather their oral history. The following interview with one Amir Tāvideh is quite suggestive:

70. Such phrases include *adām Allāh baqā'ahu* (May God prolong his presence), *dāmat ifāżātuh* (May his outpourings of wisdom and learning last), and for a dead person *ṭāba s̱arāhu* (May his dust [on his tomb and/or the dust he has become] be clean [or well-scented]).

71. When I asked a high-level Iranian official who was consulting with me about graduate studies in the early 1990s why he wanted a doctorate, he answered without hesitation: "so that people will call me āqā-ye doktor." I am happy to report that since then he has been granted that wish without having had to waste his time on obtaining a PhD.

72. Lewis R. Aiken and Richard L. Zweigenhaft, "Signature Size, Sex, and Status in Iran," *Journal of Social Psychology* 106:2 (December 1978): 273–274.

73. See Reza Arasteh, "The Character, Organization, and Social Role of the *Lutis* (*Javanmardan*) in the Traditional Iranian Society of the Nineteenth Century," *Journal of the Economic and Social History of the Orient* 4:1 (1961): 47–52.

Q: By the way, why is it that most *luṭis* have a byname (*laqab*)?

A: A title is the marker of people ... for instance Moṣṭafā Divuneh (the crazy) [was called that] because he was courageous and lionhearted; in Reżā Shah's time he pulled down a police station sign ... My own title was Tārzān.[74]

Among the lower classes, informal *laqabs*, perhaps not quite as suggestive as those of the *luṭis*, thrive even today. In 2006, an anthropologist studying pigeon fanciers (*kaftarbāzes*) in southern Tehran found that in that area, family names were mostly used for "people who had a higher level of education." In their own neighborhood, men were referred to by their forename and the honorific *Āqā* (e.g. Aḥmad Āqā), while a man from a different neighborhood was called by his forename along with a further term referring to the street where he lived, his regional background (e.g. Hādi Rashti), or his ethnicity (e.g. Dāriush Torkeh), echoes of the *nisba* and *laqab* of yore. More prosperous artisans or professionals bore bynames referring to their profession, such as Ṣādeq Āhangar (Ṣādeq the ironmonger) or Ṣādeq Ḥammāmi (Ṣādeq the bathhouse owner).[75]

The latest challenge to the fixed sequence of forename and surname registered at birth has been caused by the massive emigration of Iranians following the revolution of 1979. Throughout history, immigrants have often changed their surnames,[76] and in the United States this is actually quite easy.[77] Iranian immigrants, however, are more likely to change their first names than their family names,[78] perhaps because America has become so informal that forenames are what matter there most - not to mention the desirability of maintaining family lineages intact, although on an international scale that is rendered somewhat complicated by the fact that because the Persian language has no official transliteration into the Latin alphabet, relatives spell their names differently depending on the country to which they have emigrated.

74. Sinā Mirzā'i and Seyyed Moḥammad Ḥoseyni, *Az sargoẕasht-e luṭihā* (Tehran: Madyā, 1383/2004), 128.

75. Alexander Reddaway, "The Practice of Pigeon Flying in Southern Tehran and Its Image in Iranian Society" (MA thesis, McGill University, Institute of Islamic Studies 2007), 43.

76. On the French case see James E. Jacob and Pierre L. Horn, "*Comment vous-appelez-vous?*: Why the French Change Their Names," *Names* 46:1 (March 1998): 13–15.

77. Leonard R.N. Ashley, "Changing Times and Changing Names: Reasons, Regulations, and Rights," *Names* 19:3 (September 1971): 167–187.

78. Betty A. Blair, "Personal Name Changes among Iranian Immigrants in the USA," in Asghar Fathi, ed., *Iranian Refugees and Exiles since Khomeini* (Costa Mesa, CA: Mazda Publishers, 1991), 145–160.

Comparative Perspectives

In light of the structural similarities that were discussed in chapter 1 between Iran and a number of other post-"semicolonial" states, it is instructive to compare the Iranian experience with that of these countries, especially Turkey. At first sight it seems astonishing that the introduction of family names occurred in Iran almost a decade before it did in Turkey. In Turkey, the law abolishing titles and introducing family names was adopted by parliament on 21 June 1934. This was done in the presence of Reżā Shah, who was in Turkey on a state visit,[79] and on the occasion Turkish officials flattered their guest by pointing out that a similar law had been adopted first in Iran–which, according to a British report, filled some deputies with mirth.[80]

In fact, though, if family names were not made obligatory in Turkey until 1934, one reason may have been that state registries already existed there, unlike in Iran. These registries always recorded a person's name and his or her father's name as well as the date and place of birth or registration, but the rest of what was recorded was not standardized and could include occupation, father's job, military rank, nickname, and/or ethnic origins. And thanks to these registries, conscription had been instituted in the Ottoman Empire much earlier.

As for family names, in the rural areas of much of Anatolia "there were appellations that resembled surnames," and "it was commonly the case that a collection of agnatically related households in a village might designate themselves by a collective name."[81] Moreover, family groupings had names "composed of the putative personal name, attribute, or title of an ancestral father ... plus a suffix, '*oğlu.*'"[82] At the elite level, at the end of the nineteenth century, educated people – such as the writers and artists Halit Ziya, Mehmet Rauf, Ziya Gökalp, and Hüseyin Cahit – began using two names.[83] The concept of surnames was therefore already known when in 1926 a new civil code provided for them.

On 11 March 1933 a commission was set up to draft a name law. According to the commission's report to the Grand National Assembly, the purpose of the law was fivefold:

79. Afshin Marashi, "Performing the Nation: The Shah's Official State Visit to Kemalist Turkey, June to July 1934," in Stephanie Cronin, ed., *The Making of Modern Iran* (London: Routledge, 2003), 99–119.

80. Sir P[ercy] Loraine to Sir John Simon, December 13, 1934, E7433/7431/44; FO 371/17971.

81. Michael E. Meeker, *A Nation of Empire: The Ottoman Legacy of Turkish Modernity* (Berkeley: University of California Press, 2002), 311.

82. Ibid., 13.

83. İbrahim Aksu, *The Story of Turkish Surnames: An Onomastic Study of Turkish Family Names, Their Origins, and Related Matters* (Çanakkale: Olay Gazete Press, 2005), 4–15.

1 to eliminate bureaucratic confusion: surnames would make census taking, tax collection, conscription, schooling, and other official matters much easier, for "even if Turkish families have surnames, they do not use them";

2. to be civilized and European: "if countries all over the world have recognised the need for citizens to possess surnames, then Turkey should follows suit if it seeks to be a modern, civilised, European-style country. As well as in dress and other regulations, there is a need to identify family members with a common name the modern way.... The surname law will overcome this deficiency in our system.... It has been a tradition for centuries that every family and every individual bears a surname. We, on the other hand, have been found wanting and arrived at the situation seen today";

3. to destroy the power of the sheykhs and clans: "the clan system belongs to the Middle Ages and signifies division and separation.... It is necessary to exorcise the memory of clans and tribes.... In the East there are more than 200 clans such as the Haydaralı, the Halikanlı, the Yusufanlı etc. If we accept tribal affinity, if we do not remove these allegiances, later on many people will oppose us, saying they are Haydaralı or Yusufalı. It is necessary to abolish these at once for the sake of national unity";

4. to remove ethnic divisions; and

5. to strengthen family coherence.[84]

These motivations are remarkably similar to those enunciated by King Vajiravudh (r. 1910–1925) in 1913, when he made family names obligatory in Siam. On 22 March of that year he issued a decree announcing the awarding of family names. The preamble said that the king wished to ensure that government records of births, marriages, and deaths would be clear and reliable and that identification of individuals and their line of descent would be free from possible error. The "standard of civilization" was thereby met: "Now we have surnames and it can be said that we have caught up with people who are regarded as civilized." The decree had twenty articles that provided details: surnames were to be adopted by all Thai; the surname was to be the permanent name of the family and was to be handed down in the male line; a married woman was to bear her husband's surname; the family head, that is, the oldest living male of a family, was to choose the family name; this name had to be a suitable one in the sense that it must be in keeping with the person's position (certain names were restricted to royalty or the

84. Ibid., 21–22.

nobility and were not to be used by commoners); it should have no coarse connotations; it must not require more than ten letters to write; it must not duplicate any other surname within a given district or neighboring district; district officials were to help the people choose surnames, and, to this end, circulars were to be issued listing possible names; and names were to be registered in the district office and a certificate of registration given to the family head. The decree was to become law on July 1, 1913, and six months thereafter all heads of families were to have complied by registering a name with a district office. At the end of the six-month period, no official document was to be prepared that did not set down the surname as well as the given name of individuals mentioned in the document. Enforcement proved to be difficult. The deadlines were postponed several times, and in 1925, by the end of King Vajiravudh's reign, enforcement of the decree appeared to have been indefinitely postponed. In the countryside, in particular, it was not possible to enforce the measures, and in everyday interactions, the Thai, like the Turks, stuck to their forenames.[85]

To come back to Turkey: the name law was approved in the internal committee of the Grand National Assembly in late 1933,[86] was adopted by that body on 21 June 1934, and became law on 2 July. Like the Iranian law, the new Turkish law entrusted the male head of the household with the choice of a surname. Significantly, it stipulated that the family name be placed after the first name – which is contrary to the internal logic of Altaic languagues.[87] This decision, which was not unopposed,[88] was clearly an attempt to conform to the dominant European pattern. The law forbade the adoption of any surname that consisted of an official title or military rank or the name of a clan, foreign race, or nation; was contrary to public decency; or was repulsive or absurd.[89] In November 1934 the Grand National Assembly passed another law, prohibiting titles and honorifics such as *Ağa*, *Hacı*, *Hafiz*, *Hoca*, *Efendi*, *Bey*, *Beyefendi*, *Paşa*, *Hanım*, *Hanımefendi*, and *Hazretleri*.[90] They were replaced by only two terms, *Bay* for men and *Bayan* for women, each preceding

85. Walter F. Vella, *Chaiyo!: King Vajiravudh and the Development of Thai Nationalism* (Honolulu: The University Press of Hawaii, 1978), 129–135.

86. *Milliyet*, 13 December 1933, as quoted in *Oriente Moderno* 41:1 (January 1934): 22.

87. Cf. Hungarian and Japanese surnames, which come before the given names.

88. The onomastician Ziyaeddin Fahri Fındıkoğlu (1901–1974) publicly opposed putting the surname after the first name. Aksu, *The Story of Turkish Surnames*, 45.

89. Ibid., 33–34.

90. Meltem Türköz, *Naming and Nation-building in Turkey: The 1934 Surname Law* (New York: PalgraveMacmillan, 2018), 79–84. For a list of titles and honorifics used in late Ottoman times see Muhammad Djinguiz, "Les titres en Turquie," *Revue du monde musulman* 3 (1907): 244–258.

the name proper. But it remained common to address people by their first name + *Bey* (for men) or *Hanım* (for women): until 1950, in fact, the Istanbul telephone book was organized by alphabetical order of first names.[91]

On 15 December 1934 the Statute of Regulations (*Soyadı Nizamnamesi*) was issued as a government decree, specifying how the surname law would be enforced and carried out. It had fifty-four provisions, several of which are relevant to us here.[92] Most importantly, surnames would be taken from the Turkish language (provision 5). Centralizing states often use surnames for the purpose of nation building by outlawing reminders of languages other than the official state language,[93] and while the Turkish law here contrasts with the earlier Iranian law of 1925, which had no such provision, it parallels the Thai experience, where the numerous and influential Chinese minority was forced to adopt Thai names.[94] In the same vein, names of ethnic groups and foreign nations were forbidden (e.g. Arnavutoğlu, which refers to Albanians),[95] as were endings such as *-yan*, *-of*, *-ef*, *-viç*, *-iç*, *-is*, *-dis*, *-pulos*, *-aki*, *-zade*, *-mahmudu*, *-veled*, and *-bin* (provision 7).[96] Nor could surnames that claimed a relationship to a clan (*aşiret*) or communal group (*kabile*) be used, or later reattached (provision 8). This, too, was different from the Iranian law, which included no such provision. Finally, as in Iranian law, upon marriage a woman gave up her father's name and took her husband's (provision 17).

The more intense nationalism of the Turkish name law can be explained by the creeping dismemberment of the Ottoman Empire, which had gone on for a century, leaving Turkey's leaders with the conviction that enough was enough, the presence of several ethnic minorities (most importantly Kurds) in the Republic of Turkey notwithstanding. In addition, millions of refugees from the Balkans had to be integrated into the Turkish nation, now that the Islamic *ummah* (the larger, international community of Muslims) was no longer a referent. In Iran, by contrast, of all the peripheral forces that threatened the country's territorial integrity after World War I, only

91. Geoffrey Lewis, *Turkey*, third ed. (London: Ernest Benn Limited, 1965), 111.

92. Aksu, *The Story of Turkish Surnames*, 35–40.

93. For a discussion that includes the Turkish case see Teresa Scassa, "National Identity, Ethnic Surnames and the State," *Canadian Journal of Law and Society* 11:2 (1996): 167–191.

94. Chris Baker and Pasuk Phongpaichit, *A History of Thailand* (Second Edition) (Melbourne: Cambridge University Press, 2009), 95.

95. Not only that, but Kurds in Eastern Turkey were often assigned surnames that included the word *türk*.

96. By 1934 in Turkey Greeks, Armenians, and Jews already had recorded family names. They could change them to Turkish names, and because of social pressure many did, but some did not. Aksu, *The Story of Turkish Surnames*, 237–238.

the emirate of Muḥammara had an ethnic base, and that was easily subdued by Reżā Khan, under whom its Arabic name was changed to the Persian Khorramshahr.

The Turkish surname law went into force on 1 January 1935, and the deadline for choosing names was set for 2 July 1936. If somebody had not chosen a name, a designated authority would choose one. In the villages, officials gave names to everyone in one day; at times, as in Iran, some of these names were ridiculous.[97]

The president of Turkey, Mustafa Kemal, was far more directly affected by these changes in his country's laws than was Reżā Pahlavi, whose surname antedated the Iranian name laws. First, Mustafa Kemal changed his forename from Kemal to Kamal, arguing that it came from the Turkish *kale* (fortress) rather than from the Arabic *Kemal*. Later, however, he reverted to Kemal,[98] perhaps because he had realized that *kale* also comes from Arabic (*qilʿa*). He then asked the Grand National Assembly to confer a surname on him, and soon meetings were held around his dinner table and in the parliamentary caucus of the Republican People's Party to find a suitable family name for the president.[99] The choice was narrowed to Türkata and Türkatası, but then Üstad Naim Hazım (Onat) Bey, a prominent philologist and deputy from Konya, suggested that the old title Atabey (in Persian Atābak), meaning "teacher and/or advisor of the ruler," be used as a model, yielding Atatürk (father of the Turks), a name that everyone liked and that was conferred on the president by the Grand National Assembly on 24 November 1934.[100] In early December the deputy from Kocaeli, İbrahim Süreyya, proposed that no one else could ever carry this "patronym par excellence," as Emmanuel Szurek has aptly called it, for which the head of state rewarded him with the surname Yığıt, meaning "the brave."[101] Thereafter, Turks chose family names for themselves,[102] except that, unlike in Iran, a number of booklets with lists of surnames were published by both state and non-state preses,[103] many of

97. Ibid., 23 and 229.

98. Ibid., 24.

99. Proposed surnames included Etel-Etil, Etealp, Korkut, Arız, Ulaş, Yazır, Emen, Çoğaş, Salır, Begit, Ergin, Tokuş, and Beşe. M. Şakir Ülkütaşır, "Wie wurde Atatürk dieser Familienname gegeben und wer hat ihn gefunden?" *Cultura Turcica* 8/9/10 (1971–1973): 35.

100. Ibid., 36 and Robert F. Spencer, "The Social Context of Modern Turkish Names," *Southwestern Journal of Anthropology* 17:3 (Autumn 1961): 206–207.

101. Emmanuel Szurek, "Appeler les Turcs par leur nom. Le nationalisme patronymique dans la Turquie des années 1930," *Revue d'histoire moderne & contemporaine* 60:2 (2013): 33 and 33 n66.

102. Schimmel, *Herr "Demirci" heißt einfach "Schmidt"*, 46–70; and Spencer, "The Social Context": 212–217.

103. Türköz, *Naming and Nation-building in Turkey*, 95–99.

them neologisms with highly nationalistic and/or heroic overtones, from which people could choose – for which process there was no Iranian equivalent. This explains the profusion of people named Yilmaz (dauntless), Kaya (rock), or Demir (steel).[104]

The manner in which family names were introduced in both Iran and Turkey, i.e. by parliamentary legislation, contrasts sharply with the case in Siam, where they were introduced in 1913 by personal initiative of the king, at a time when Siam was still an absolute monarchy. Until then, like Iranians and Turks, common Thai people had only had a given name, while elites "were identified by an elaborate system of titles made up of ranks and conferred names, [these titles functioning] in much the same way as personal names." King Vajiravudh personally chose surnames for members of his Court and even fixed their transliteration in the Latin alphabet. The pre-constitutional state of the Thai polity can be seen in the fact that while Turkish and Iranian laws tried to equalize the status of male citizens, in Siam King Vajiravudh developed systems for differentiating social classes by means of the surnames.[105]

Given the intense nationalism that motivated the Iranian and Turkish governments in the 1920s and 1930s, a nationalism that all too often begat a desire to purge the "national culture" of "foreign elements," comparing the two countries' approaches to family names yields a few ironies. Before assuming the family name Atatürk, Mustafa Kemal was sometimes called Ali Rıza Bey zade Mustafa Kemal,[106] i.e., Mustafa Kemal son of Ali Rıza. Ali Rıza combines the name and the title of the eighth Twelver Shiite Imam, who is buried in Iran, and as a forename is very popular in Iran – so popular, in fact, that each of the two Pahlavi Shahs gave it to his second son. Meanwhile, Reżā Shah's father's name was 'Abbās 'Ali Khān, but he was known as Dādāsh-Beyk: a compound of two Turkish nouns.[107] It is even more ironic that (as noted earlier) the Turkish words *Āqā* and *Khānom* became the only permissible forms of address for men and women in Iran the year after the same terms, spelled *Ağa* and *Hanım* in modern Turkish, were outlawed in Turkey (which does not mean that they disappeared from everyday usage).

As we saw earlier, when Turkish legislation outlawed "foreign" elements in family names, they meant Arabic and Persian words and names as well, although in practice such a ban could not be sustained and there are still plenty of Turkish names and surnames that contain Arabic and Persian

104. Szurek, "Appeler les Turcs par leur nom": 27–28.
105. Vella, *Chaiyo!*, 132.
106. Spencer, "The Social Context": 209.
107. Niyāzmand, *Reżā Shāh*, 29.

elements; to this day, for instance, there is a Mahmutzade family in Istanbul.[108] However, someone who wishes to become a naturalized citizen of Turkey is required to adopt a Turkish forename and a Turkish surname.[109]

108. Aksu, *The Story of Turkish Surnames*, 229.

109. This happened in 1982 to Fariborz Farhangi, a longtime Iranian resident in Istanbul, who became Ferit Ferengil upon becoming a Turkish citizen. Personal e-mail communication from him, 21 July 2015.

CONCLUSION

The story of the establishment of Iran's new onomastic regime in the second and third decades of the twentieth century once more proves that many of the reforms commonly identified with the rule of Reżā Shah actually originated in the transitional period between the Constitutional Revolution in 1906 and his ascent to the throne in the first half of the 1920s.[1] The 1925 change of dynasty was the smoothest in Iranian history, as Yamin al-Dowleh, a son of Nāṣer al-Din Shah, observed upon being honored at the Court of Reżā Shah.[2] One element of continuity was the activities of the parliament, which in those days played a significant role in legislation, although it was admittedly not fairly elected. The state-building initiatives of successive governments after 1906 ended up superseding the social functions of the ulema in a number of domains, thus begetting a certain secularization of Iranian society.[3]

Modernist Iranian patriots, like their Turkish, Siamese, and Chinese counterparts, craved the recognition of the Western powers and felt humiliated by the Europeans - as shown by the fact that a third-rate French novel was cited in the Iranian parliament in support of the abolition of titles. On the day that Reżā Pahlavi, then still the prime minister, personally went to the Iranian parliament to punish those who opposed his plans, he angrily pounded the table with his fist and expostulated: "if today Europeans have changed their view about Iran, it is because Reżā Māzandarāni is working in Iran."[4] The most tangible token of such recognition would be European acquiescence to the abolition of the capitulations, which the Iran government finally obtained in 1928.

In implementing the reform of naming practices, the Iranians treaded

1. This point is also forcefully made in regard to the judicial reforms in Hadi Enayat, *Law, State, and Society in Modern Iran: Constitutionalism, Autocracy, and Legal Reform, 1906–1941* (New York: Palgrave Macmillan, 2013).

2. Qahramān Mirzā Sālur, ʻEyn al-Salṭaneh, *Ruznāmeh-ye khāṭerāt-e ʻEyn al-Salṭaneh (Qahramān Mirzā)*, ed. Masʻud Sālur and Iraj Afshār, volume 9 (Tehran: Asāṭir, 1379/2000), 7438.

3. This theme is developed in Arang Keshavarzian, "Turban or Hat, Seminarian or Soldier: State Building and Clergy Building in Reza Shah's Iran," *Journal of Church and State* 45:1 (Winter 2003): 81–112.

4. Yaḥyā Dowlatābādi, *Tārikh-e ʻaṣr-e ḥāżer yā jeld-e chehārom-e Ḥayāt-e Yaḥyā*, volume 2 (Tehran: Ebn-e Sinā, 1331/1952), 359.

more cautiously than did the Turks, much as the Iranians also showed greater restraint in matters of language purification.[5] Perhaps this was because they felt more secure: after all, Iran had survived World War I with its external borders intact. In Iran, state building took precedence over nation building; in Kemalist Turkey, it was exactly the other way around. Turkey had inherited the state apparatus of the Ottoman Empire, while in Iran such an apparatus had to be set up almost from scratch. In Iran, meanwhile, the population remained the same before and after the regime change of 1925, and the "Iranian nation," in the sense of fellow citizens of a state, could be taken as a given.

The *Memalik-i Mahruse-i Osmaniye* and the *Mamālek-e Mahruseh-ye Irān* (Guarded Domains of the Ottomans and Guarded Domains of Iran), as the Ottoman Empire and the Iran of the Qājārs were called, respectively, were both multiethnic empires, and while it is true that the states that succeeded them, the Turkish Republic and the Pahlavi state, were both committed to the negation of multiethnicity and the propagation of a monolithic ethnic nationalism premised upon the derivation of a "national" feeling from a "national" language, the multiethnic cultural substance of Iranian society survived more openly than did its counterpart in Turkey. Many Iranian modernists held the "foreign" origin of the Qājārs, who had been players on Iran's political scene for a mere half a millennium, against them and hailed Reżā Shah as a pure Iranian, but in fact Reżā Shah's mother was a (Muslim) Georgian and his Queen (the mother of his Crown Prince) an ethnic Turk from the Caucasus, both their families having fled to Iran to escape the Russian advance. Reżā Shah's spoken Turkish was good enough that he and Atatürk needed no interpreter when they met in 1934. Moreover, his eldest daughter married into a family that took the name Ātābāy – the very term that inspired Naim Hazım Bey to coin the name Atatürk.

Although the Iranian state did try to propagate the use of Persian at the expense of other languages, Iran, unlike Turkey, never had a "language law" prohibiting the use of any language other than the official one. In practice, if not in theory, therefore, everyday Iranian culture continued to regard ethnic cultures as part of the national self, a tendency that found its onomastic expression in the continued use of Turkish first names (Allāhverdi, Ḥoseyn-Qoli, Jeyrān) along with family names containing the Arabic definite article *al-* or the Turkish suffix *-chi* or *-lu*.[6] The 1937 bylaws mandating the dropping

5. John R. Perry, "Language Reform in Turkey and Iran," in Touraj Atabaki and Erik J. Zürcher, eds., *Men of Order: Authoritarian Modernization under Atatürk and Reza Shah* (London: I.B. Tauris, 2004), 238–259.

6. Which in the Turkish of Turkey becomes *-lu*, *-lü*, *-li*, or *-lı*, depending on the requirements of vowel harmony.

of "foreign" words in surnames obviously did not apply to Turkish or Arabic words. Today one of Iran's most celebrated artists bears the unambiguously Turkish name of Āydin Āghdāshlu, while a celebrated Assyrian theater director of the 1960s and 1970s was called Assurbanipal Babilla.

Perhaps the fact that the official inscription on Iranian passports was *Empire de l'Iran* until 1979 expressed something more than just the vanity of a ruler who wanted to be addressed as "Your Imperial Majesty."[7] Although nation building in Iran aimed to create a nation-state based on the Persian language, Iran was in some, admittedly limited, ways also a "state-nation," by which I mean a state in which a civic and territorial idea of nationhood coexists with the acceptance of ethnic diversity, as in India.[8] The cohesion of this civic nation was enhanced by the name laws, standardizing the form but not the content of citizens' appellations. Together, the name laws, the conscription laws, and the abolition of slavery created a more egalitarian society, in which (male and Muslim) citizens enjoyed the same rights and duties.[9] The advent of the Islamic Republic reversed this progress towards more legal equality, for instance by registering the religion of "recognized religious minorities" in their identity papers, as well as providing for conversion to Islam while denying the right of conversion to Muslims who might want to convert to another religion.

There is an old saying that Arabic persuades, Persian flatters, and Turkish commands. The flowery titles and honorifics common in late-nineteenth- and early-twentieth-century Iran seem to bear out this observation. The social practices and cultural values they expressed were already being denounced by modernist critics in the nineteenth century, but it took the thwarted republicans of 1924 to mount a determined assault on them. Social practices and cultural values cannot be changed by law or decree, of course, and so it was only in the aftermath of the revolution of 1978–1979 that a more egalitarian, occasionally even coarse, mode of interacting appeared among the citizenry of Iran.[10]

7. Cf. Jean-François Bayart, "Republican Trajectories in Iran and Turkey: a Tocquevillian Reading," in Ghassan Salamé, ed., *Democracy without Democrats?* (New York: St. Martin's Press, 1994), 282–301, in which the author argues that in some ways it was the establishment of the Islamic Republic that did for Iran what the establishment of republican government had done for Turkey, superficial resemblances between the policies of Atatürk and Reżā Shah notwithstanding.

8. I am using the definition of "state-nation" offered in Juan J. Linz, Alfred Stepan, and Yogendra Yadav, "The Rise of 'State-Nations,'" *Journal of Democracy* 21:3 (July 2010): 50–68.

9. Yann Richard, "La fondation d'une armée nationale en Iran," in Yann Richard, ed., *Entre l'Iran et l'Occident* (Paris: Editions de la Maison des Sciences de l'Homme, 1989), 56–57.

10. Mohammad Hossein Keshavarz, "Forms of Address in Post-Revolutionary Iranian Persian: A Sociolinguistic Analysis," *Language in Society* 17 (1988): 565–575.

BIBLIOGRAPHY

Abrahamian, Ervand. *Iran Between Two Revolutions*. Princeton: Princeton University Press, 1982.

Abuẕarjomehri, Mahasti. "Alqāb-e zanān dar 'aṣr-e Qājār (bā takkiyeh bar asnād-e Ārshiv-e Melli). *Faṣlnāmeh-ye Ārshiv-e Melli* 2:2 (Summer 1395/2016): 36–51.

Afkhami, Amir Arsalan. "Compromised Constitutions: The Iranian Experience with the 1918–1919 Influenza Pandemic." *Bulletin of the History of Medicine* 77:2 (Summer 2003): 367–392.

Afshār, Iraj. "Shesh Moshir al-Dowleh." *Bokhārā* 75 (Farvardin-Tir 1389/ March-June 2010): 542–554.

——— ed. *Nāmehhā-ye Pāris az Moḥammad-e Qazvini beh Seyyed Ḥoseyn-e Taqizādeh*. Tehran: Nashr-e Qaṭreh, 1384/2005.

Afshār, Iraj and 'Ali Moḥammad Honar, eds. *Masā'el-e pārisiyeh: Yāddāshthā-ye 'Allāmeh Moḥammad-e Qazvini*, volume 2. Tehran: Enteshārāt-e Mowqufāt-e Doktor Maḥmud Afshār, 1390/2011.

Aghagolzadeh, Ferdows and Hiwa Asadpour. "A Critical Discourse Analysis of Address in Persian." *International Journal of Humanities* 18:1 (2011): 135–160.

Aiken, Lewis R. and Richard L. Zweigenhaft. "Signature Size, Sex, and Status in Iran." *Journal of Social Psychology* 106:2 (December 1978): 273–274.

Aksu, İbrahim. *The story of Turkish surnames: an onomastic study of Turkish family names, their origins, and related matters*. Çanakkale: Olay Gazete Press, 2005.

Alamuti, Moṣṭafā. *Irān dar 'aṣr-e Pahlavi*, volume 12. London: Book Press, 1992.

Alford, Richard D. *Naming and Identity: A Cross-Cultural Study of Personal Naming Practices*. New Haven: HRAF Press, 1987.

'Ālikhāni, 'Ali-Naqi, ed. *Yāddāshthā-ye 'Alam*, volume 6, *1355-1356*. Bethesda: Ibex, 2008.

'Āqeli, Bāqer. *Ruzshomār-e tārikh-e Irān az mashruṭeh tā enqelāb-e eslāmi*. Tehran: Nashr-e Goftār, 1369/1990.

Arasteh, Reza. "The Character, Organization, and Social Role of the *Lutis* (*Javanmardan*) in the Traditional Iranian Society of the Nineteenth Century." *Journal of the Economic and Social History of the Orient* 4:1 (1961): 47–52.

[Arfa', Reżā]. Le Prince Mirza Riza Khan Daniche Arfa-od-Dovleh. *Poésie et Art Persans à Monaco*. Monte Carlo: Imprimerie du "Petit Monégasque", 1919.

Ashley, Leonard R.N. "Changing Times and Changing Names: Reasons, Regulations, and Rights." *Names* 19:3 (September 1971): 167–187.

Ashraf, Aḥmad. "Laqab va 'onvān." In *Dar zamineh-ye irānshenāsi*, edited by Changiz Pahlavān, 267–303. Tehran: Published by the editor, 1368/1989.

Ayubi, Vaḥid, ed. *Zendegi va gozideh-ye āsār-e Ḥasan-e Moqaddam*. Tehran: Ketābsarā-ye Nik, 1385/2006.

Āzari, Reżā, ed. *Dar takāpu-ye tāj va takht: Asnād-e Abu al-Fatḥ Mirzā Sālār al-Dowleh Qājār*. Tehran: Enteshārāt-e Sāzmān-e Asnād-e Melli-ye Irān, 1378/1999.

'Ażod al-Dowleh, Shāhzādeh Solṭān Aḥmad Mirzā. *Tārikh-e 'Ażodi*, edited by Doktor 'Abd al-Ḥoseyn Navā'i. Tehran: Bābak, 2535/1976.

Bābā Safari. *Ardabil dar gozargāh-e tārikh*, volume 2. Ardabil: Islamic Azad University Press, 1991.

Baker, Chris and Pasuk Phongpaichit. *A History of Thailand*. 2nd ed. Melbourne: Cambridge University Press, 2009.

Banani, Amin. *The Modernization of Iran*. Stanford: Stanford University Press, 1961.

de la Barre de Raillicourt, Dominique. *Les titres authentiques de la noblesse en France*. Paris: Perrin, 2004.

Başgöz, Ilhan. "The Meaning and Dimension of Change in Personal Names in Turkey." *Turcica* 15 (1983): 201–218.

Bast, Oliver. "La mission persane à la Conférence de Paix en 1919: une nouvelle interprétation." In *La Perse et la Grande Guerre*, edited by Oliver Bast, 375–426. Tehran/Paris: Institut Français de Recherche en Iran/ Peeters, 2002.

——. "Putting the Record Straight: Vosuq al-Dowleh's Foreign Policy in 1918/19." In *Men of Order: Authoritarian Modernization under Atatürk and Reza Shah*, edited by Touraj Atabaki and Erik J. Zürcher, 260–281. London: I.B. Tauris, 2004.

Bāstāni Pārizi, Moḥammad Ebrāhim. *Talāsh-e āzādi*. Tehran: Enteshārāt-e Khorram, 1379/2000.

Bayart, Jean-François. "Republican Trajectories in Iran and Turkey: a Tocquevillian Reading." In *Democracy without Democrats?*, edited by Ghassan Salamé, 282–301. New York: St. Martin's Press, 1994.

Bayāt, Kāveh. *Shuresh-e 'ashāyeri-ye Fārs: sālhā-ye 1307–1309 H.Sh*. Tehran: Nashr-e Noqreh, bā hamkāri-ye Enteshārāt-e Zarrin, 1365/1986.

Bayly, C.A. *The Birth of the Modern World 1780-1914*. Oxford: Blackwell, 2004.

Beeman, William O. *Language, Status, and Power in Iran*. Bloomington: Indiana University Press, 1986.

Behniyā, Doktor ʻAbd al-Karim. *Nām: pazhuheshi dar nāmhā-ye irāniyān-e moʻāṣer*. Tehran: Enteshārāt-e Shahid Farhād Reżā, 1360/1981, 1374/1995.

Belgorodskii, N.A. "Sotsial'nyi element v persidskikh imenakh, prozvishchakh, titulakh i familiiakh." In *Zapiski Instituta Vostokovedeniia Akademii Nauk*, volume 1, 213–242. Leningrad: Izdatel'stvo Akademii Nauk SSSR, 1932.

Blair, Betty A. "Personal Name Changes among Iranian Immigrants in the USA." In *Iranian Refugees and Exiles since Khomeini*, edited by Asghar Fathi, 145–160. Costa Mesa, CA: Mazda Publishers, 1991.

Blücher, Wipert von. *Zeitenwende in Iran: Erlebnisse und Beobachtungen*. Biberach an der Riss: Koehler & Voigtländer, 1949.

Bosworth, C.E. "The Titulature of the Early Ghaznavids." *Oriens* 15 (1962): 210–233.

Bromberger, Christian. "Pour une analyse anthropologique des noms de personnes." *Langages* 66 (June 1982): 103–124.

de Bruijn, J.T.P. "The name of the poet in classical Persian poetry." In *Proceedings of the Third European Conference of Iranian Studies*, Part 2: *Mediaeval and Modern Persian Studies*, edited by Charles Melville, 45–56. Wiesbaden: Dr. Ludwig Reichert Verlag, 1999.

Bulliet, Richard W. "First Names and Political Change in Modern Turkey." *International Journal of Middle East Studies* 9:4 (November 1978): 489–495.

Busse, Heribert. *Chalif und Grosskönig: Die Buyiden im Iraq (945–1055)*. Wiesbaden: Franz Steiner, 1969.

"The Cataloguing of Persian Works: Iranian Personal Names: Their Characteristics and Usage." *Unesco Bulletin for Libraries* 14:5 (September-October 1960): 205–209, 232.

Çelebi, Evliya, ed. and trans. Robert Dankoff and Robert Elsie. *Evliya Çelebi in Albania and Adjacent Regions (Kosovo, Montenegro, Ohrid)*. Leiden: Brill, 2000.

Centlivres, Pierre. "Noms, surnoms et termes d'adresse dans le nord afghan." *Studia Iranica* 1:1 (1972): 89–102.

Chehabi, Houchang E. "Staging the Emperor's New Clothes." *Iranian Studies* 26:3–4 (Summer/Fall 1993): 209–233.

Chehabi, H. E. "The Reform of Iranian Nomenclature and Titulature in the Fifth Majles." In *Convergent Zones: Persian Literary Tradition and the Writing of History: Studies in Honor of Amin Banani*, edited by Wali Ahmadi, 84–116. Costa Mesa, CA: Mazda Publishers, 2012.

Christensen, Arthur. *L'Iran sous les Sassanides.* Copenhagen: Ejnar Munksgaard, 1944.

Churchill, Rogers Platt. *The Anglo-Russian Convention of 1907.* Cedar Rapids, IA: The Torch Press, 1939.

Cook, Andrew. *Cash for Honours: The True Life of Andrew Gregory*. Stroud: History Press, 2008.

Coston, Baron [François Gilbert] de. *Origine, étymologie & signification des noms propres et des armoiries.* Paris: Chez Aug. Aubry, éditeur, 1867.

Cronin, Stephanie. *The Army and the Creation of the Pahlavi State in Iran, 1910–1926.* London: I.B. Tauris, 1997.

——. "Conscription and Popular Resistance in Iran, 1925–1941." *International Review of Social History* 43:3 (1998): 451–471.

Dashti, 'Ali. *Ayyām-e maḥbas.* Tehran: Enteshārāt-e Asāṭir, 1380/2001.

Delmond, Paul. "De l'imposition des noms de personnes aux africains." *Bulletin de l'Institut Français d'Afrique Noire* 15:2 (1953): 453–460.

Devos, Bianca. *Presse und Unternehmertum in Iran: die Tageszeitung Ittilā'āt in der frühen Pahlavī-Zeit.* Würzburg: Ergon Verlag, 2012.

Dietrich, Albert. "Zu den mit *ad-Dīn* zusammengesetzten islamischen Personennamen." *Zeitschrift der deutschen morgenländischen Gesellschaft* 110:1 (1960): 45–54.

Djinguiz, Muhammad. "Les titres en Turquie." *Revue du monde musulman* 3 (1907) : 244–258.

Dowlatābādi, Yaḥyā. *Tārikh-e 'aṣr-e ḥāżer yā Ḥayāt-e Yaḥyā,* volume 4. Tehran: Ebn-e Sinā, 1331/1952.

Effendi, Karagueuz [Jacques de Morgan]. *Le Chah du Mahboulistan: Histoire Orientale.* Paris: "Le Livre", 1923.

Ehsani, Kaveh. "Oil, State and Society in Iran in the Aftermath of the First World War." In *The First World War and its Aftermath*, edited by Thomas Fraser, 191–212. London & Chicago: Gingko Library Press, 2015.

Enayat, Hadi. *Law, State, and Society in Modern Iran: Constitutionalism, Autocracy, and Legal Reform, 1906–1941.* New York: Palgrave Macmillan, 2013.

Estayngās [Steingass], F. *Farhang-e Estayngās: Fārsi-engelisi.* Tehran: Sherkat-e Sahāmi-ye Enteshārāt-e Khᵛārazmi, 2535/1976.

E'temād al-Salṭaneh, Moḥammad Ḥasan Khān. *Ketāb al-ma'āṯer va l-āṯār.* Tehran: Dār al-Ṭabā'eh-ye Dowlati, 1306/1927.

——. *Ruznāmeh-ye khāṭerāt-e E'temād al-Salṭaneh,* edited by Iraj Afshār. Tehran: Amir Kabir, 1389/2010.

Ettehadieh, Mansoureh. *The Lion of Persia: a Political Biography of Prince Farmān-Farmā.* Cambridge, MA: Tŷ Aur Press, 2012.

Farrokh, Mehdi. *Khāṭerāt-e siyāsi-ye Farrokh, Mo'taṣem al-Salṭaneh*. Tehran: Sāzmān-e Enteshārāt-e Jāvidān, n.d.

Fragner, Bert. "World War I as a Turning Point in Iranian history." In *La Perse et la Grande Guerre*, edited by Oliver Bast, 443–447. Tehran/Paris: Institut Français de Recherche en Iran/Peeters, 2002.

Garcin de Tassy, [Joseph-Héliodore-Sagesse-Vertu]. *Mémoire sur les noms propres et les titres musulmans*. Paris: Imprimerie Impériale, 1854.

Gevergiz, Hānibāl. *Tārikhcheh-ye dāneshkadeh-ye pezeshki-ye Orumiyeh*. Enteshārāt-e Dāneshgāh-e Olum-e Pezeshki-ye Tehrān, n.d.

Ghani, Cyrus. *Iran and the Rise of Reza Shah: From Qajar Collapse to Pahlavi Rule*. London: I.B. Tauris, 1998.

Gheissari, Ali. "Merchants without Borders: Trade, Travel and a Revolution in Late Qajar Iran (the Memoirs of Hajj Mohammad-Taqi Jourabchi, 1907–1911)." In *War and Peace in Qajar Persia: Implications past and present*, edited by Roxane Farmanfarmaian, 183–212. London: Routledge, 2008.

——. "Constitutional Rights and the Development of Civil Law in Iran." In *Iran's Constitutional Revolution: Politics, Cultural Transformations and Transnational Connections*, edited by H. E. Chehabi and Vanessa Martin, 74–76. London: I.B. Tauris, 2010.

Gong, Gerrit W. *The Standard of 'Civilization' in International Society*. Oxford: Clarendon Press, 1984.

Habibi, Nader. "Iranian Names." *International Journal of Middle East Studies* 24:2 (May 1992): 253–260.

Ḥejāzi, Moḥammad. *Mihan-e mā*. Tehran: Enteshārāt-e Vezārat-e Farhang, 1338/1959.

Hughes, James Pennethorne. *How You Got Your Name: The Origin and Meaning of Surnames*. London: Phoenix House, 1959.

Jacob, James E. and Pierre L. Horn. "*Comment vous-appelez-vous?*: Why the French Change Their Names." *Names* 46:1 (March 1998): 3–28.

Jones, Russell. *Chinese Names: The Traditions Surrounding the Use of Chinese Surnames and Personal Names*. Selangor: Pelanduk Publications, 1997.

Kasravi, Aḥmad. *Khᵛāharān va dokhtarān-e mā*. Bethesda, MD: Iranbooks, 1371/1992.

Katouzian, Homa. *The Political Economy of Modern Iran: Despotism and Pseudo-Despotism, 1926–1979*. London: Macmillan, 1981.

——. "The Campaign Against the Anglo-Iranian Agreement of 1919." *British Journal of Middle Eastern Studies* 25:1 (1998): 5–46.

——. *State and Society in Iran: The Eclipse of the Qajars and the Emergence of the Pahlavis*. London: I.B. Tauris, 2006.

Kauz, Ralph. *Politische Parteien und Bevölkerung in Iran: die Hezb-e Demokrat-e Iran und ihr Führer Qavamo s-Saltana*. Berlin: Klaus Schwarz, 1995.

Kayalı, Hasan. "Liberal Practices in the Transformation from Empire to Nation-State: The Rump Ottoman Empire, 1918–1923." In *Liberal Thought in the Eastern Mediterranean: Late 19th Century until the 1960s*, edited by Christoph Schumann, 175–194. Leiden: Brill, 2008.

Kazemzadeh, Firuz. *Russia and Britain in Persia, 1864-1914: A Study in Imperialism*. New Haven: Yale University Press, 1968.

Kekule, Dr. Stephan. *Über Titel, Ämter, Rangstufen und Anreden in der offiziellen osmanischen Sprache*. Halle: Druck und Verlag von C.A. Kaemmeren & Co., 1892.

Keshavarz, Mohammad Hossein. "Forms of address in post-revolutionary Iranian Persian: a sociolinguistic analysis." *Language in Society* 17 (1988): 565–575.

Keshavarzian, Arang. "Turban or Hat, Seminarian or Soldier: State Building and Clergy Building in Reza Shah's Iran." *Journal of Church and State* 45:1 (Winter 2003): 81–112.

Kluge, Inge-Lore. "Die heutigen japanischen Familiennamen und ihre Entstehung in historischer Sicht." In *Erlanger Familiennamen-Colloquium: Referate des 7. interdisziplinären Colloquiums des Zentralinstituts*, edited by Rudolf Schützeichel and Alfred Wendehorst, 121–128. Neustadt an der Aisch: Degener, 1985.

Kowner, Rotem, ed. *The Impact of the Russo-Japanese War*. London: Routledge, 2007.

Kurzman, Charles. *Democracy Denied, 1905-1915: Intellectuals and the Fate of Democracy*. Cambridge, MA: Harvard University Press, 2008.

Lebra, Takie Sugiyama. *Above the Clouds: Status Culture of the Modern Japanese Nobility*. Berkeley: University of California Press, 1993.

Lefebvre-Teillard, Anne. *Le nom: droit et histoire*. Paris: Presses universitaires de France, 1990.

Lenin, V. I. "On the Slogan for the United States of Europe." In *Collected Works*, volume 21, 339–343. New York: International Publishers, 1967.

Lewis, Geoffrey. *Turkey*. 3rd ed. London: Ernest Benn Limited, 1965.

Linz, Juan J., Alfred Stepan, and Yogendra Yadav. "The Rise of 'State-Nations'." *Journal of Democracy* 21:3 (July 2010): 50–68.

Litten, Wilhelm. "Persische Familiennamen." *Der Neue Orient* 6:5 (1920): 196–198.

Machalski, Franciszek. "Die Personennamen der Schuljugend von Iran." *Folia Orientalia* 12 (1970): 155–163.

Maʻādikhᵛāh, Ḥojjat al-Eslām ʻAbd al-Majid. *Jām-e shekasteh: Khāṭerāt.* Tehran: Markaz-e Asnād-e Enqelāb-e Eslāmi, 1382/2003.
Madelung, Wilferd. "The Assumption of the Title Shāhānshāh by the Būyids and 'The Reign of the Daylam (*Dawlat Al-Daylam*)'." *Journal of Near Eastern Studies* 28:2 (April 1969): 84–108.
Maḥbubi Ardakāni, Ḥoseyn. *Tārikh-e mo'assesāt-e tamaddoni-ye jadid dar Irān*, volume 2. Tehran: Mo'asseseh-ye Enteshārāt va Chāp-e Dāneshgāh-e Tehrān, 1376/1998.
Mahdavi Dāmghāni, Aḥmad. "Tārikhcheh-ye maḥżar va daftar-e asnād-e rasmi." *Bokhārā* 89–90 (Mehr-Dey 1391 / September-December 2002): 122–137.
Maḥmud Khān Malek al-Shoʻarā Ṣabā. "Tartib-e alqāb." *Farhang-e Irānzamin* 19 (1352/1973): 62–88.
Majd al-Eslām Kermāni, Aḥmad. "Kharid va forush-e manāṣeb va alqāb dar Irān." *Yād* 18 (1382/2003): 309–318.
Majmuʻeh-ye qavānin-e mowżuʻeh va moṣavvabāt-e dowreh-ye panjom-e taqniniyeh. Tehran: Maṭbaʻeh-ye Majles, n.d.
Majmuʻeh-ye qavānin-e mowżuʻeh va masā'el-e moṣavvabeh-ye dowreh-ye sheshom-e taqniniyeh. Tehran: Maṭbaʻeh-ye Majles, n.d.
Makki, Ḥoseyn. *Tārikh-e bist-sāleh-ye Irān*, volume 2, *Moqaddamāt-e taghyir-e salṭanat.* Tehran: Nashr-e Nāsher, 1362/1983.
——. *Tārikh-e bist-sāleh-ye Irān*, volume 3, *Enqerāż-e Qājāriyeh va tashkil-e selseleh-ye diktātori-ye Pahlavi.* Tehran: Nashr-e Nāsher, 1382/1983.
Marashi, Afshin. "Performing the Nation: The Shah's Official State Visit to Kemalist Turkey, June to July 1934." In *The Making of Modern Iran*, edited by Stephanie Cronin, 99–119. London: Routledge, 2003.
Markaz-e Asnād-e Enqelāb-e Eslāmi, ed. *Haftād sāl khāṭereh az Āyat A... Seyyed Ḥoseyn Bodalā.* Tehran: Markaz-e Asnād-e Enqelāb-e Eslāmi, 1378/1999.
Martin, Vanessa. "Mudarris, Republicanism and the Rise to Power of Riza Khan, Sardar Sipah." *Bulletin of the British Society for Middle Eastern Studies* 21:2 (1994): 200–211.
Mashruḥ-e moẕākerāt-e majles-e showrā-ye eslāmi, dowreh-ye dovvom. Tehran: n.p., 1363/1984.
Matine-Daftary, Dr. Ahmad Khan. *La suppression des capitulations en Perse: L'ancien régime et le statut actuel des étrangers dans l'Empire du "Lion et Soleil".* Paris: Presses universitaires de France, 1930.
Matini, Jalāl. "Baḥs̱i darbāreh-ye sābeqeh-ye tārikhi-ye alqāb va ʻanavin-e ʻolamā dar maẕhab-e shiʻeh." *Irānshenāsi* 1:4 (Summer 1983): 560–608.
Maugard, Antoine. *Remarques sur la noblesse: dédiées aux assemblés provinciales.* Paris: Chez Lamy et Gattey, 1788.

Meeker, Michael E. *A Nation of Empire: The Ottoman Legacy of Turkish Modernity*. Berkeley: University of California Press, 2002.

Memar-Sadeghi, Abdolmajid. "Changing Personal Names and Titles in Written Farsi, 1921–1978: A Sociolinguistic Study with Pedagogical Implications." PhD Thesis, University of Illinois at Urbana-Champaign, 1980.

Menashri, David. *Education and the Making of Modern Iran*. Ithaca, NY: Cornell University Press, 1992.

Millspaugh, A.C. *The American Task in Persia*. New York and London: The Century Co., 1915.

Mirfendereski, Guive. *The Privileged American: The U.S. Capitulations in Iran 1856–79*. Costa Mesa, CA: Mazda Publishers, 2014.

Mirshekāri, 'Abbās. *Tabār-shenāsi-ye ḥoqūq-e s̱abt-e aḥvāl: moshtamal bar: qavānin, moqarrarāt va ārā-ye vaḥdat-e raviyeh dar ḥowzeh-ye ḥoqūq-e s̱abt-e aḥvāl az āghāz tā konun*. Tehran: Enteshārāt-e Jāvdāneh, 1393/2014.

Mirzā Ṣāleḥ, Gholām Ḥoseyn ed. *Reżā Shāh: Khāṭerāt-e Soleymān-e Behbudi, Shams-e Pahlavi, 'Ali-ye Izadi*. Tehran: Tarḥ-e Now, 1372/1993.

Mirzai, Behnaz A. "African Presence in Iran: Identity and its Reconstruction in the 19th and 20th Centuries." *Revue Française d'Histoire d'Outremer* 89, Nos. 336–337 (2002): 229–246.

Mirzā'i, Sinā and Seyyed Moḥammad Ḥoseyni, *Az sargoẕasht-e luṭihā*. Tehran: Madyā, 1383/2004.

Moḥiṭ Ṭabāṭabā'i, Moḥammad. "Shukhi va jeddi." *Yaghmā* 18:1 (1344/1965–66): 38–46.

Moin, Baqer. *Khomeini: Life of the Ayatollah*. London: I.B. Tauris, 2009.

Mojtahed-Zadeh, Pirouz. *The Amirs of the Borderlands and Eastern Iranian Borders*. London: Urosevic Foundation, 1995.

Morādiniyā, Moḥammad Javād, ed. *Khāṭerāt-e Āyat Allāh Pasandideh*. Enteshārāt-e Ḥadis̱, 1374/1995.

——, ed. *Ruznāmeh-ye khāṭerāt-e Seyyed Moḥammad Kamareh'i*, volume 2, *moqaddamāt-e kudetā-ye sevvom-e Esfand*. Tehran: Shirāzeh, 1382.

Mori, Kenji. "The Development of the Modern *koseki*." In *Japan's Household Registration System and Citizenship:* Koseki, *Identification and Documentation*, edited by David Chapman and Karl Jakob Krogness, 59–75. London: Routledge, 2014.

Mostowfi, 'Abd Allāh. *Sharḥ-e zendegāni-ye man*, volume 1. Tehran: Ketābforushi-ye Moḥammad 'Ali Forughi, 1324/1945.

Motadel, David. "Iran and the Aryan myth." In *Perceptions of Iran: History, Myths and Nationalism from Medieval Persia to the Islamic Republic*, edited by Ali M. Ansari, 119–145. London: I.B. Tauris, 2014.

Mozākerāt-e Majles-e Showrā-ye Melli, dowreh-ye panjom. Tehran: Edāreh-ye ruznāmeh-ye rasmi-ye keshvar-e shāhanshāhi-ye Irān, n.d.
Najjāri, Mahdi. *Chegunegi-ye e'tā-ye alqāb-e moshābeh dar dowreh-ye Qājār (Motāle'eh-ye mowredi bar ru-ye laqab-e Moshir al-Dowleh).* Tehran: Nedā-ye Tārikh, 1394/2015.
Nasiri-Moghaddam, Nader. *L'archéologie française en Perse et les antiquités nationales (1884–1914).* Paris: Éditions Connaissances et Savoirs, 2004.
Nāṭeq, Homā. *Irān dar rāhyābi-ye farhangi 1834–1848.* London: Payām, 1988.
Nāṭeq, Mirzā Javād. "Khāṭerāt-e man." Unpublished manuscript.
Nautré, Sylvie. *Le nom en droit comparé.* Frankfurt: Peter Lang, 1977.
Navādeh-ye Mohalleb pesar-e Moḥammad pesar-e Shādi. Ed. Seyf al-Din Najmābādi and Zigfrid Veber [Siegfried Weber]. *Mojmal al-tawārikh wa l'qeṣaṣ.* Edingen-Neckarhausen: deux mondes, 2000.
Neẓām al-Molk Ṭusi. Ed. 'Abbās Eqbāl. *Siyāsatnāmeh.* Tehran: Enteshārāt-e Asāṭir, 1372/1993.
Niyāzmand, Doktor Reżā. *Reżā Shāh az tavallod tā salṭanat.* Tehran: Enteshārāt-e Jāme'eh-ye Irāniyān, 2002/1381.
Noiriel, Gérard. "The Identification of the Citizen: The Birth of Republican Civil Status in France." In *Documenting Individual Identity: The Development of State Practices in the Modern World,* edited by Jane Caplan and John Torpey, 28–48. Princeton: Princeton University Press, 2001.
Oberling, Pierre. *The Qashqā'i Nomads of Fārs.* The Hague: Mouton, 1974.
Oppenheim, L. *International Law: A Treatise.* London: Longman's, 1905.
Parsi, Rouzbeh. *In Search of Caravans Lost: Iranian Intellectuals and Nationalist Discourse in the Inter-war Years.* Lund: Media-tryck, 2009.
Penot, D. *Le Dictionnaire des Noms et Prénoms arabes.* Lyon: ALIF éditions, 1996.
Perreau, E.-H. *Le Droit au nom en matière civile.* Paris: Librairie de la Société du Recueil Sirey, 1910.
Perry, John R. "*Mīrzā, Mashtī* and *Jūja Kabāb*: Some Cases of Anomalous Noun Phrase Word Order in Persian." In *History and Literature in Iran: Persian and Islamic Studies in honour of P.W. Avery,* edited by Charles Melville, 213–228. London: British Academic Press, Cambridge University, 1990.
———."Language Reform in Turkey and Iran." In *Men of Order: Authoritarian Modernization under Atatürk and Reza Shah,* edited by Touraj Atabaki and Erik J. Zürcher, 238–259. London: I.B. Tauris, 2004.
———. "New Persian: Expansion, Standardization, and Inclusivity." In *Literacy in the Persianate World,* edited by Brian Spooner and William L. Hanaway, 70–94. Philadelphia: University of Pennsylvania Press, 2012.
Plutschow, Herbert. *Japan's Name Culture: The Significance of Names in a Religious, Political and Social Context.* Sandgate: Japan Library, 1995.

"A propos de la suppression officielle des titres honorifiques." *Revue du monde musulman* 61 (1925): 171–172.

Qalafi, Moḥammad Vaḥid. *Majles va nowsāzi dar Irān (1302–1311 h. sh.)*. Tehran: Nashr-e Ney, 1379/2000.

Qānun-e madani. Tehran: Mo'asseseh-ye maṭbu'āti-ye Amir Kabir, 1333/1954.

Qominezhād, Mahdi. *Alqāb va manāseb-e 'aṣr-e Qājāri va asnād-e Amin al-Żarb: Yādegāri az Asghar Mahdavi*. Tehran: S̱orayyā, 1388/2009.

Rāhnamā-ye estefādeh az ṣurat-e mashruḥ-e moẕākerāt-e majles-e barrasi-ye nahā'i-ye qānun-e asāsi-ye jomhuri-ye eslāmi-ye Irān. Tehran: Edāreh-ye koll-e omur-e farhangi va ravābeṭ-e 'omumi-ye majles-e shurā-ye eslāmi, 1368/1989.

Rajabzādeh, Doktor Aḥmad. *Taḥlil-e ejtemā'i-ye nāmgoẕāri*. Tehran: Ravesh, 1378/1999.

Rastegar, Nosratollah. "Iranische Personennamen neupersischer Überlieferung: Ein Beitrag zu einigen kritischen Werkausgaben klassischer Epen." In *Proceedings of the Second European Conference of Iranian Studies*, edited by Bert G. Fragner, Christa Fragner, Gherardo Gnoli, Roxane Haag-Higuchi, Mauro Maggi, and Paola Orsatti, 581–582. Rome: Istituto per il Medio Oriente ed Estremo Oriente, 1995.

Rāzi, Ḥājj Moḥammad Sharif. *Ganjineh-ye dāneshmandān*. Tehran: Ketābforushi-ye Eslāmiyeh, 1352–54.

Reddaway, Alexander. "The Practice of Pigeon Flying in Southern Tehran and its Image in Iranian Society." MA thesis, McGill University, Institute of Islamic Studies 2007.

Rennick, Robert M. "On the Right of Exclusive Possession of a Family Name." *Names* 32:2 (June 1984): 138–155.

Richard, Yann. "La fondation d'une armée nationale en Iran." In *Entre l'Iran et l'Occident*, edited by Yann Richard, 43–60. Paris: Editions de la Maison des Sciences de l'Homme, 1989.

———. *Répertoire prosopographique de l'Iran moderne: "Rejâl" (Iran, 1800–1953)*. Paris: Sorbonne Nouvelle, 2012.

Richter-Bernburg, Lutz. "Amīr-Malik-Shāhānshāh: 'Aḍud ad-Daula's Titulature Re-Examined." *Iran* 18 (1980): 83–102.

Ringer, Monica M. *Pious Citizens: Reforming Zoroastrianism in India and Iran*. Syracuse: Syracuse University Press, 2011.

Rostam al-Ḥokamā' (Moḥammad Hāshem Āsaf). *Rostam al-tavārikh*, edited by Moḥammad Moshiri. Tehran: Chāp-e Tābān, 1348/1969.

Sālur, Qahramān Mirzā. *Ruznāmeh-ye khāṭerāt-e 'Eyn al-Salṭaneh (Qahramān Mirzā)*, edited by Mas'ud Sālur and Iraj Afshār, 10 volumes. Tehran: Asātir, 1374–1380/1995–2001.

"Salverte, Eusebius" [Anne Joseph Eusèbe Baconnière Salverte]. *History of the Names of Men, Nations, and Places in their Connection with the Progress of Civilization*, trans. L.H. Mordacque. London: John Russell Smith, 1862.

Scassa, Teresa. "National Identity, Ethnic Surnames and the State." *Canadian Journal of Law and Society* 11:2 (1996): 167–191.

Schimmel, Annemarie. *Islamic Names*. Edinburgh: Edinburgh University Press, 1989.

——. *Herr „Demirci" heißt einfach „Schmidt": Türkische Namen und ihre Bedeutung*. Cologne: Önel-Verlag, 1992.

Schmitt, Rüdiger. *Das iranische Personen-Namenbuch: Rückschau, Vorschau, Rundschau*. Vienna: Verlag der Österreichischen Akademie der Wissenschaften, 2006.

Schütz, Joseph. "Russische Familiennamen." In *Erlanger Familiennamen-Colloquium: Referate des 7. interdisziplinären Colloquiums des Zentralinstituts*, edited by Rudolf Schützeichel and Alfred Wendehorst, 41–47. Neustadt an der Aisch: Degener, 1985.

Scott, James C., John Tehranian, and Jeremy Mathias. "The Production of Legal Identities Proper to States: The Case of the Permanent Family Name." *Comparative Studies in Society and History* 44:1 (January 2002): 4–44.

Scott, James C. *Seeing Like a State: How Certain Schemes to Improve the Human Condition Have Failed*. New Haven: Yale University Press, 1998.

Sellheim, Rudolf. "„Familiennamen" im islamischen Mittelalter." *Orientalia Suecana* 33–35 (1984–1986): 375–384.

Shahri, Ja'far. *Gushehhā'i az tārikh-e ejtemā'i-ye Tehrān-e qadim*. Tehran: Mo'in, 1370/1991.

Shaji'i, Zahrā. *Nokhbegān-e siyāsi-ye Irān az enqelāb-e mashruṭiyat tā enqelāb-e eslāmi*, volume 3, *Hey'at-e vazirān-e Irān dar 'aṣr-e mashruṭiyat*. Tehran: Enteshārāt-e Sokhan, 1372/1993.

Shamsā, Moḥammad Reżā and Ṭāhereh Mehrvarzān, eds. *Khāṭerāt-e Āyat Allāh 'Ali Āl-e Esḥāq*. Tehran: Enteshārāt-e Markaz-e Asnād-e Enqelāb-e Eslāmi, 1385/2006.

Shaw, Stanford J. "The Ottoman Census System and Population, 1831–1914." *International Journal of Middle East Studies* 9:3 (October 1978): 325–338.

Shuster, W. Morgan. *The Strangling of Persia*. Washington, DC: Mage, 1987.

Siddiq, Mohammad Yusuf. *Epigraphy and Islamic Culture: Inscriptions of the Early Muslim Rulers of Bengal (1205-1494)*. New York: Taylor & Francis, 2016.

Şimşek, Veysel. "The First 'Little Mehmeds': Conscripts for the Ottoman Army, 1826–53." *Osmanlı Araştırmaları / The Journal of Ottoman Studies* 44 (2014): 265–311.

Smith, E. C. *The Story of Our Names*. New York: Harper and Brothers Publishers, 1950.

Soleymāni, Karim. *Alqāb-e rejāl-e dowreh-ye Qājāriyeh*. Tehran: Nashr-e Ney, 1379/2000.

Solṭāni, Moḥammad 'Ali. *Tārikh-e mofaṣṣal-e Kermānshāhān*, volume 4. Tehran: Moḥammad 'Ali Solṭāni, 1373/1994.

Spencer, Herbert. *The Principles of Sociology*, volume 2. New Brunswick, NJ: Transaction Publishers, 2002.

Spencer, Robert F. "The Social Context of Modern Turkish Names." *Southwestern Journal of Anthropology* 17:3 (Autumn 1961): 205–218.

Szurek, Emmanuel. "Appeler les Turcs par leur nom. Le nationalisme patronymique dans la Turquie des années 1930." *Revue d'histoire moderne & contemporaine* 60:2 (2013): 18–37.

"Tartib-e alqāb." In *Farhang-e Irānzamin* 19 (1352/1973): 62–88.

"Tashkhiṣ va tarqim-e alqāb." In *Farhang-e Irānzamin* 19 (1352/1973): 49–61.

Tchen, Yaotong. *De la disparition de la jurisdiction consulaire dans certains pays d'Orient*. Paris: Les Presses Modernes, 1931.

Tomasson, Richard F. "The Continuity of Icelandic Names and Naming Patterns." *Names* 23:4 (December 1975): 281–289.

Türköz, Meltem. *Naming and Nation-building in Turkey: The 1934 Surname Law*. New York: PalgraveMacmillan, 2018.

Ülkütaşır, M. Şakir. "Wie wurde Atatürk dieser Familienname gegeben und wer hat ihn gefunden?." *Cultura Turcica* 8/9/10 (1971–73): 32–38.

Uskowi, Omid and A. Reza Sheikholeslami. "Impact of the Constitutional Revolution on the Development of the Modern State in Iran." In *Convergent Zones: Persian Literary Tradition and the Writing of History: Studies in Honor of Amin Banani*, edited by Wali Ahmadi, 117–148. Costa Mesa, CA: Mazda Publishers, 2012.

Vanderlinden, Jacques. *The Law of Physical Persons (Art. 1-393). Commentaries upon the Ethiopian Civil Code*. Addis Ababa: Faculty of Law, Haile Sellassie I University, 1969.

Vella, Walter F. *Chaiyo!: King Vajiravudh and the Development of Thai Nationalism*. Honolulu: The University Press of Hawaii, 1978.

Vroonen, Eugène. *Les Noms des personnes dans le monde: anthroponymie universelle comparée*. Brussels: Éditions de la Librairie Encyclopédique, 1967.

Weber, Max. *Economy and Society*, trans. Guenther Roth and Claus Wittich. Berkeley: California University Press, 1978.

Winichakul, Thongchai. "The Quest for 'Siwilai': A Geographical Discourse of Civilizational Thinking in the Late Nineteenth and Early Twentieth-Century Siam." *The Journal of Asian Studies* 59:3 (August 2000): 528–549.

Yao, Kouo Kin. *La Chine et les capitulations*. Nancy: Imprimerie Georges Thomas, 1938.
Yārshāṭer, Eḥsān. "Nāmhā-ye irāni." *Irānshenāsi* 1:2 (Summer 1368/1989): 324–329.
Yemane, Elias. *Amharic and Ethiopic Onomastics: A Classic Ethiopian Legacy, Concept, and Ingenuity*. Lewiston: The Edwin Mellen Press, 2004.
Zand Moqaddam, Maḥmud. *Ḥekāyat-e Baluch*, volume 4: *Kordhā, Englishā, Baluchhā*. Tehran: Published by the author, 1371/1992.
Żiyāyi, Moḥammad Reża. "'Ostād' beh cheh kasi miguyand? (Dar bāb-e eghrāq dar alqāb)." *Bokhārā* 109 (Āẕar-Dey 1394): 363–366.
Zirinsky, Michael. "Reza Shah's abrogation of capitulations, 1927–1928." In *The Making of Modern Iran: State and Society Under Riza Shah 1921-1941*, edited by Stephanie Cronin, 81–98. London: Routledge, 2003.

Encyclopedias and Dictionaries:

Encyclopaedia Aethiopica
Encyclopaedia Iranica
Encyclopaedia of Islam
Loghatnāmeh-ye Dehkhodā
Wikipedia (Spanish)
Wikipédia (French)

Newspapers and Journals:

Eṭṭelā'āt
Irān
Majalleh-ye rasmi-ye vezārat-e 'adliyeh
New York Times
Niru va rāst
Ra'd

Index